GATHER THE FRAGMENTS

From the time, many years ago, when my mother read to me before bed, I have loved beautiful stories. This is a beautiful story, a story of many stories made of hope. It is Maureen O'Brien's own story which, as I read it, kept conjuring up Emily Dickinson's luminous words, "Hope is the thing with feathers / That perches in the soul" and whose song "never stops" and never "asked a crumb of me." And with each individual story I could feel the singing bird's feathers lifting and lifting me as I read.

These stories could do that because they were not sentimental or detached from life as we all experience it which involves our own share of pain and suffering, loneliness, and despair. O'Brien's story of stories lifts hope's feathers because her words incarnate and make real these words she quotes from Thich Nhat Hanh: "Because I suffer, I need love. Because you suffer, you need love. Because we suffer, we know we have to offer each other love." And love is what O'Brien offers us in this gathering up of the fragments of the loves she has known.

—Fr. Murray Bodo, OFM, author of
Francis: The Journey and the Dream

With an eye for metaphor and an unpretentious but contemplative voice, Maureen O'Brien's writing is a celebration of the sacredness to be found in the minutiae of our regular old lives. *Gather the Fragments* paints pictures that I will return to again and again.

—Shannon K. Evans, author of
Rewilding Motherhood and *Luminous*

gather the fragments

My Year of Finding
God's Love

Maureen O'Brien

franciscan
media®
Cincinnati, Ohio

2/23

To the Little Ray
of Sunshine!
with much thanks
for your gift
to me —
light in a
hard time —
love Maureen

Some names and identifying characteristics have been changed.

The author wishes to thank the Conference on Christianity and Literature for their Travel Grant, which allowed for travel to Italy, and Arte Studio Ginestrelle Writers Residency in Assisi, Italy, which provided time, space, and beauty to write. Thanks to Father Bill Bowdoin for permission to include his homily, and to Sister Grace Coffey for sharing the miracles of The Shrine of the Little Flower. Gratitude to Christopher Roque for the inclusion here of his haiku and to Flemin Haynes (T.S.) for his poem. Deep appreciation to Anna Symington for proofreading.

Library of Congress Control Number: 2022948762
ISBN 978-1-63253-423-1

Cover and book design by Mark Sullivan

Published by Franciscan Media
28 W. Liberty St.
Cincinnati, OH 45202
www.FranciscanMedia.org

Printed in the United States of America.

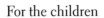

For the children

Contents

Introduction

This book is born of three words, *gather the fragments*, and I invite you here to share them, no matter what you believe, what you've rejected, what you are suspicious of, and especially, what you long for. I stumbled upon the phrase one day when I was writing for Franciscan Media's online resource *Pause+Pray*. As I sought inspiration and ideas, flipping through the New Testament, I saw this: *Gather the fragments.*

I read what came before, curious about what framed it, and landed right in the center of the miracle of the multiplication of the loaves, when Jesus is preaching before a large and hungry crowd.

One of his disciples said to him, "There is a boy here who has five barley loaves and two fish, but what good are these for so many?" Jesus said, "Have the people recline." Now there was a great deal of grass in that place. So the men reclined, about five thousand in number. Then Jesus took the loaves, gave thanks, and distributed them to those who were reclining, and also as much fish as they wanted. When they had their fill, he said to his disciples, "Gather the fragments left over, so that nothing will be wasted." So they collected them and filled twelve wicker baskets with the fragments from the five barley loaves that had been more than they could eat. (John 6:8–14)

What floored me was that these were the words of Jesus, and though I've attended church for so many years, I never heard them. Did I? They sounded so present-day. I thought of my own life, and the struggles of my loved ones, how we have spent so much time struggling to make peace with our emptiness, our brokenness.

Having wandered unawares into this story, I began writing meditations on these words. I've consequently been dazzled, moved, and transformed. I am not the person I was a year ago. Studying this miracle, repeatedly coming back to *gather the fragments*, these three words, daydreaming about them, carrying them everywhere in my pocket, has opened up more possibilities than I ever imagined. I have more love and trust, and quite honestly, the grief of the spaces left behind from disease, the years of being unheld, the loneliness I have always carried—all gone. This is a miracle. I cannot speak for anyone else, I can only share my own vulnerable truth that this year of ardent fragment gathering has filled me with an unshakeable certainty that God's love and abundance is here, right now, alongside us and in us.

I am not out to defend any miracle as true, real, possible, or logical. As I have read and researched the stories of miracles, for me, they have gotten completely out of hand. Winged things, they fly around, dart here and there, land, show their gorgeous magic, then fly away into the clouds, camouflaged. Just when I think I've heard them all, another one appears. Many are outlandish. In fact, most of them are.

That's what makes them miracles.

They encompass, by their very nature, the words *abundance* and *gratitude*. But these words are thrown around ceaselessly and everywhere, to the point where their meaning has been washed away. Here, I want to take them back into their full vibrancy. I believe that if we find and feel the wonder it redefines the broken world. Yes, a broken world of inescapable sorrow, despair, and horror, but also a world bursting with possibility and grace if we see that we're given not just what we need, but maybe even more.

The Hunger

Fishing Poles in Spring

Surviving a New England winter takes strength. And I am in southern New England; spring comes entire months earlier for me than it does for my brother, sister, and mother in Maine. The early signs that fill us with relief that we did, in fact, make it, are sort of clichéd, I guess. The garden: yellow forsythia popping on delicate long arcs; the beginning buds of the lilac, so new when they first emerge they're monochrome; and of course even months before the final snow squall, the green tips of snowdrops and crocus and daffodils emerge in the sun-warmed corners by our front doors.

But the most hopeful signs of spring are the fishing poles and little tackle boxes of the fishermen and fisherwomen that appear around the lake. They are solitary as the Great Blue Herons, who are also fishing. There's an expectancy in the air, coming from the lake itself, as if it, too, is eager to begin again as a body entirely made of water, freed of its tight skin of ice.

There's silence. The songbirds aren't migrating through yet, just the geese, and the woodpeckers hammering the soft, rotten trees that have uprooted and fallen over in the winter. The fishermen and fisherwomen are a contemplative lot. When they pass others on their way to their chosen spot, they nod, rarely grin, make a bit of eye contact, but don't mutter more than "hello." They aren't there to make new friends, and so what? They've come for something profoundly simple: to stare at the surface of water and ponder what's under it. Casting the whole afternoon and leaving when it's so dark the lake has become only sound.

They want to stare at the water and think of nothing but fish. Of the hope of fish. The pull of fish on their line. In all my years of silently passing by the fishing poles, I have never seen a single person catch something in this lake. Perhaps my timing has been off, but not once have I seen this. It makes me love these fishermen and women more. Because really, isn't hope what it's all about? They bring *me* hope. Every spring I come around from the Upper Trail Head, and there they are: hope is the shape of a human holding a fishing pole.

I go to sleep thinking of their reflection in the water, the squiggly ripples of poles, and I awake to light my candles and find the day's entry in my daily reader, *The Book of Awakening* by Mark Pepo. "We live like hungry fishermen: sewing and casting our nets, though we never really know what they will catch, never really know what will feed us until it is brought aboard."[1] There are fish, somewhere, moving through the lake, swimming within our dreams. And we're all around that shore, together, either full from our last meal or longing for the next.

Shards

Faith can so often be invisible, clear as a morning whisper. Sometimes I just want to touch it. This is why I'm drawn to archeology, and how I fell in love with the big fat fish. He was unearthed in 2015 by archeologists in Israel who found a mosaic on the floor of the fifth-century Byzantine "Burnt Church." That name alone calls to me. *Burnt Church.* Torched in the seventh century, the sacred space destroyed, the mosaic had been protected, paradoxically, by the cinders of the roof that sifted down and left a heavy cover of ash. The tiles on the ancient floor tell the story of the Miracle of the Loaves and Fishes, spirals of bread atop baskets, fruit, feathers, birds, fish.

Of course, the news of a dig of this magnitude spread around the world, and scholars began to hypothesize about its meaning, searching for clues. Is this charred site perhaps the actual, true place where the miracle occurred? Not, as is commonly believed, across Lake Kinneret at Tabha? No one knows. They studied Scripture and matched it with images of the floor, considering the fish of the region, the split dorsal fins of Nile perch, the single fins of the tilapia from the Sea of Galilee. Me? I don't need any historical confirmation to appreciate the gift of this reveal. What I would have given to be one of those conservators kneeling in the sun, cleaning away the dust of sixteen hundred years, and freeing the pomegranates underneath with a brush.

The fish I now feel is "mine" is the fattest of them all, with a face so cute, so expressive, he's smiling. His eye has one gray stone in the center, surrounded by seven circles of widening gray and beige tiles, a few orange, a few russet. The scholarly articles judge the craftsmanship of his tilework "mediocre." Not great art. This makes me become defensive of him and love him even more. Yes, the history of tilework is beyond any schooling I have. Even if he *is* ordinary and average, this little guy waited under ashes for sixteen centuries.

But I know what it is to wait for a long time to be found, covered in darkness. I began drinking at thirteen. I spent the following nine years in a haze of self-loathing, nakedness, wandering, and blackouts. A blackout is drinking and drugging so much you don't remember where you were, who you were with, or what you had done. For several years, I would lose up to nine hours at a time. Last remembering 8:00 p.m. and then coming to just before dawn, unsure of what transpired.

I have details, many sharp pieces, of these years of ugliness and violence. Somehow, I managed to graduate from college with a BA in philosophy and religion. Those studies of God gave me a lifeline, I believe. I had moved to Hartford and sat in my car in a parking lot one night, eating fast food, unwrapping the paper around a Filet-O-Fish in my lap. I thought, "I'm going to end it." And I could feel, at that moment, a dead-end. The end of the road. There was nothing more for me. Nothing left.

I was a body made up of pieces of despair. I could not bear to live with the weight of the shame crushing my bones. My addictions had shattered me. I'd been shattering myself. I figured why not just die, let it all turn to chalk. And by "it all," I mean what remained of my life. I knew the wind that would carry my dust away would eventually not even remember it once held me.

It wasn't a voice that came to me: it was words like on an electronic marquee. The letters went gliding, made of golden bare light bulbs. The words that moved right to left read, "There's something more."

I knew I was being given a message. I felt it in the void of my heart. In my ribcage where a hunger hung that had no beginning and no end.

The next morning I got out the phone book and in the Yellow Pages I looked up therapists. The very first one was a woman named Lois Aaron, listed alphabetically. She had not just one A, but two, putting her at the top of the list. I called her. I was twenty-two. I thought my life was over until that message came. *There's something more.* I made an appointment. In the months with her that followed, I began to see I was very sick. A drunk. An addict. I went to Twelve-Step meetings and stopped doing everything on July 21, 1983. I have not had a drink or drug since. I got married and had two children, a daughter and a son. My son's name reflects the woman who helped me save my life. His middle name is Aaron: it means *shining light.*

There are reams of details left out, whole novels. But I don't think the details matter. All that matters to me is that in order to keep the darkness at bay, I have turned to God for thirty-nine years. I know that using any substance would kidnap me right back into the blackness, and I have fallen in love with the light. All the light. I want to stay in it. I don't ever want to leave it.

Perhaps it is corny to be writing about the Loaves and Fishes and to recount my lowest hour of bottoming out in a city parking lot in my broken-down car that didn't even open on the driver's side. Every time I got into that car, I did it through the passenger's door. Sitting in the fluorescent light with a fifty-nine-cent sandwich in my hands, too poor to get a side of fries or a soda with it, and seeing that this is the beginning of my journey with God's miracles. The thing is, miracles can be kind of corny.

And so I celebrate the Big Fat Fish they unearthed on the floor of the church after all those years. I see who we are together. Both of us are made of shards, yet somehow, still here. Somehow still whole.

Riding the River

The Farmington River rushed high the other day, about the width of a three-lane highway, moving at a good pace after a weekend of heavy rain. I spotted a single male Mallard duck with a glistening emerald-green head. Usually, the ducks are in a group of pairs along the muddy edges. He came around a tight bend alone, about eight feet from shore, where the current was the fastest, and the surface the glassiest.

He was clearly just riding the river. I burst out laughing because he was such a tiny creature surrounded by all that water, all those trees and sky, and I could tell he felt really good. He had no intention of stopping or changing his mind. Clearly, it was just so much fun. There was no need to turn around or to fly away. He kept gliding along as if—well, as if he were part of the river. Which he was.

I kept watching until he slid out of sight beyond the farthest turn. I was sad to see him go, but he was on a mission. And this is what struck me: from the moment I spied that duck, I loved him. It made no sense. I stood wondering if this is how God viewed me. Was I like that, just moving along, loved from a riverbank, and I didn't even know it?

A melody sprang from within, matched perfectly with the lyrics. I had not thought of this song, in all honesty, in several decades. We sang it at the 10:00 a.m. folk Mass when I was a child. *Whatsoever you do to the least of my brothers, that you do unto me.* I would say that the duck qualifies as the "least of my brothers." All alone in the tranquility of the woods, my connection to nature pointed me to how I love, how I might be loved.

The heart is the heart, joyous and free. It makes no sense that I loved that little duck. Love just is. I'm dumbfounded by the mystery of it all. I'm reminded again that delight and beauty are right here. He's a *duck*. Not as cherished as a trilling lake loon, not sonnet-worthy like a duet of white swans. Though some might dismiss him as underwhelming and ordinary, he showed me possibilities. With a cap of iridescent feathers, he rode that river for all he was worth.

The Firefly

It's late July. The Northeast is rolling with the peapod-scent of cornstalks rising and clouds reflect with perfect symmetry in the stillness of the reservoirs. Two of my friends have shared with me their epiphanies of a sort, of seeing fields of nighttime fireflies, one in the state of New York, and the other in Massachusetts. *Magical. Breathtaking. That many fireflies, hundreds, it was dazzling.* I long to behold this, and as I drive past farms and uncut fields at night, I slow down and search for them. I, too, want so many fireflies switching their lights on and off in front of me that I gasp. I always want more. But I cannot find them anywhere.

Now it's one o'clock in the morning and I've stayed up too late writing. I slip into bed, and pull the chain on my bedside lamp. At the exact moment I begin to let go into sleep, the plush gray-black of my room is suddenly aglow and my room changes color. An orb of emerald green surrounds a tiny luminescent center. There's a firefly in my room! Right above me! I can't believe it. How did it get in? I do have a slight bend in the metal frame of my window screen, a slip of an opening. But where did it come from? I haven't seen a single one in my backyard.

It blinks above me, and I'm amazed at how its light fills up the entire room. One perfect firefly. I struggle to stay awake with it, to celebrate the two of us being together, but I can't. I fade away from its glow. In the morning, of course, the firefly is nowhere to be found. Yet I feel changed by its flight. I think about the fragments of the loaves, how it symbolizes God's care and protection of us, how we say *give us this day our daily bread* because we always seem to be worrying, to want more and more. Like the wish for a whole field of lights. But what if, sometimes, the abundance *isn't* in the numbers, the amount? That what we need is already near? That one little firefly found me, burning brighter than I had ever known a firefly could burn.

Fairy Lights

I sit with mothers under an open porch, not far from the river, up on the ridge. We can't see it, but we sense the water, seated as we are under the flightpath of the geese and herons. The topic is trust. As we grip our coffee mugs, the dusk slowly seeps into night. Our faces fade away, paled by one pillar candle in the middle of the table.

The fairy lights come on overhead, smaller than Christmas tree lights, strings crisscrossing on the ceiling. Somehow they've survived many seasons, delicate in their beauty but strong in persistent light.

Last December we huddled by the fire pit out in the yard, freezing, and I remember seeing them switch on in the bitter winter night, wondering how they could keep going through such severe temperature changes. Simple, cheap, solar bulbs from the place up the street that sells the cheapest of goods, Ocean State Job Lot.

Saturday night after Saturday night, whether we are sweating with August humidity or shivering with January wind, just when someone is sharing about gratitude, frustration, fears for our grown children, powerlessness over their paths and their choices and their pitfalls, sharing about an aspect of being a mother that we keep locked in our hearts, there comes a moment when the darkness has grown, and the little lights switch on.

No sound, no warning, no way of knowing when precisely they will join us, but there they are, suddenly above.

These fairy lights were never meant to last outside throughout the repeating four seasons. And yet again, they blink above, with Veronica talking to Yasmine and me of her grief but also of trying to have the best day she could have. Our coffee grows cold and the night air cools and the wick softly glows; on the whisper of the winds, the scent of sugared citrus wafts from the center sinkhole of the candle.

Our kids are in their twenties and thirties. Life keeps coming at them hard, as life does. As women in our fifties and sixties, we're getting tired. How do we detach from their terrors and tumultuous events? What is it to be a mother of adults? It's an invisible job. Everyone focuses on the time of pregnancy through a child turning eighteen, but the love is just as fierce and bottomless and baffling beyond that. With older children, we realize the full scope of the world of being human. A list of the hardships isn't what is needed here. What's needed is women like us telling the truth of love.

That love is even deeper than the day we first gathered them in our arms and looked into their eyes, birth-cloudy. Fully grown, they're the same people. They inherited the same generations of pain, confusion, and lies that *we* inherited from our parents (all the blessings too, but here I'm focusing on the tender-to-the-touch aspects of the human). And our children inherited even one more layer: *our* brokenness, too. And our partner's. A staggering fact that will only be quelled with compassion for ourselves and for them.

Yasmine asks, "How do we pull together all these fragments? This and this! The pieces of our children's lives. How do we pull them together and make them whole? We want peace in our lives. But sometimes none of it is peaceful."

The strands of lights are not enough to fully illuminate our faces, they blur as we keep sharing, our voices clear, like the cicadas calling to one another in the trees. We're the mothers, the mothers of adult children, singing through the night, heard but not seen.

Crocs

I watched my daughter, Madeline, walk down the street with her two little dogs, her hair jet black, newly dyed, piled atop her head, her confident stride, the dogs prancing happily alongside on their leashes, sniffing the crabgrass.

At the sight of her little Crocs, I felt such overwhelming love for her. A tenderness. She is a woman of thirty-one, but I felt that familiar essence of her, all her ages put together. She moved ahead of me, down the sidewalk, not knowing I was swept up in the love, pride, devotion, and poignancy. She was simply doing what dog owners do, exercising Morty and Hudson. But I felt the radiance of her beautiful spirit.

And she had no idea.

Is God's love like this, magnified?

Her "aloneness" has touched my heart ever since her beloved King Henry died. He was the most regal cat; a long-haired, orange-and-white Norwegian Forest cat who slept within the circle of her arms for seven years. She's cried and cried since he died of cancer in the spring.

After the walk we climbed the stairs up to her third-floor apartment and ordered take-out, waiting contentedly until our bags of food arrived. How blessed I am with this daughter, and the squeaking of plastic lids lifted off the Styrofoam containers. Eating while watching *The Walking Dead*. Just being together as our favorite characters try to outwit the encroaching zombies. Pausing the TV, we discuss whether now-wise, badass Carol and greasy, traumatized, good-hearted Daryl could ever be romantically together, the possibilities of them finding love.

I think of my daughter's ability to love. Her love of animals, how we stopped in the parking lot to stare at the toad whose skin blended in perfectly with the pebbled surface. Later by the pond of the Congregational Church across the street, she looked up with love at the heron that flew overhead. But most of all her maternal love of the boys she took care of at the group home. There's Ree, who will text the smiling sun emoji when he is hungry and she sends him a Domino's pizza. There's Giovante, she helps him pay his phone bill and recently found him a perfect forty-inch, flat-screen TV at Savers.

Freddie FaceTimed her as another tense episode of zombies limping and approaching began, and we paused the show while they laughed about the crazy fashions they adore. Freddie talked about Rolex watches and she said she wanted to treat herself to that pair of Prada boots (she didn't). Then it got serious. They discussed his aunt's recent death; the auntie who tried to raise him until she got sick with MS, years back, and then he disappeared into the foster care system at thirteen.

"Do you want me to go with you to the funeral?" Madeline asked. She knows him very well, both his fears of attachment, and his longing for it. He didn't say he wished for her to be alongside him with a direct yes.

Just, "OK Maddie, I'll hit you up tomorrow."

The Offering

Sea Glass Children

Josiah

Above all else, it is the miracle of children who bring forth more miracles. "There is a boy here who has five barley loaves and two fish" (John 6:9-10). It was one child who gave what he had, who held the possibility by choosing to share, beginning the entire feast.

Yesterday I got to walk with Josiah. I don't know him well and was surprised that he wanted to walk. He's failing and will have to attend summer school in order to graduate, and I am not really sure he's going to get out anytime soon. I had him on Zoom for many months, and he never once showed his face. Just a blank screen with his name. With his deep voice and edgy attitude, he sounded older, filled out, and close to manhood. One day a new kid showed up in my class. Not much taller than I am, skinnier than me. He had on a sapphire-satin do-rag, staring at me with eyes shaped like two sideways mandorlas above his face mask.

"Guess who I am," he said softly.

I had to laugh. "Wait. No. *You're* Josiah?"

He nodded.

What I know about Josiah is this. The only writing he did all year were these words: "I've been broken / into many pieces / too many pieces to count." The outside of Josiah is smooth as sea glass. He's deeper brown than a lot of the other kids of color, with a symmetry to his face that is rare, born of the fact that he doesn't have many facial expressions. He doesn't say much, but when I ask him questions, and give him a bit of a pause, he will answer. I tease him now, and have given him the nickname "Mr. Sea Glass."

"I called home one day when you weren't coming to school much. Your mom answered and said she couldn't talk because she had a baby in the tub. Do you have a sibling?"

He looks at me with that steady gaze, his eyes with the centers a bottomless, round brown. I feel like I am seeing down into him. He pauses.

"Yeah. That's my brother. He's two."

He says nothing more. I wait, too. I often get the kids to open up by talking about their nicknames, because they release a whole other interior world. "Well, he probably can't say your name at that age, so what does he call you?"

Again the pause. "Jo-Jo."

He doesn't blink often, stares, makes no unnecessary movement. He's the opposite of fidgety: he's weighed down, has a flow, as if underwater.

The thing about teaching in the middle of a pandemic, with most kids not coming to school and learning online, is that I know my few students now by their silhouettes. I now recognize who it is by the shape they make at the end of the empty hallways. The outlines of bodies, the pace they move at, the length of the stride. Josiah walks like an old man. There's no other way to describe it. His skinny legs are bent, his spine curved slightly. If you didn't know it was an eighteen-year-old, you'd think he is in his seventies, an old dude in decent shape for his age. I joked with him one day, "You walk like an old man."

"Everyone says that." No smile, nothing. Just the facts.

So yesterday when I asked, I was surprised he chose to spend time with me. Walking around our school is underwhelming, to put it mildly.

We have the gorgeous Byzantine-influenced blue dome with gold stars of the Colt Firearms Building, of course. We never tire of looking at it. But otherwise it's the wasted parking lot on one side, empty because no one comes into the city to work at Insurity anymore. There's a bus stop shelter where not a single person has waited all year. The dim winter sun glows through the plastic shell. The sprayed-painted red and black graffiti looks like Japanese calligraphy. Another parking lot for Colt and the people who live in apartments upstairs from our school. They all have jumpy pedigree dogs, and the small patches of grass inside oval curbs are brown from all the dog pee.

Josiah and I have nowhere to go but around the deserted city blocks. The one coffee shop is still closed, windows covered in brown paper. Our one food truck is gone. The Urban Gourmet Food Truck used to park by a tree with a trunk so monstrous it doesn't even seem possible that it exists in the acres of pavements and brick. I've measured the tree with students, and it takes three kids with arms wide open to encircle it.

All winter throughout the pandemic I'd take the kids out for a mask break, and as we turned west down Huyshoppe Avenue, the wind picked up bringing us aromatic gusts of the lunch menu that day, and we collectively made guttural noises of how much we all desired that food. Then we'd laugh at how beastly we sounded, half-filled with delight ignited by the steaming, spicy food, and half-filled with despair that we were all so worn out and hungry and because of strict food allergy policies at our school, we couldn't eat a single bite of it.

The last time I got the BangBang Shrimp from the food truck, Chef Charles seemed so sad. Yet he still doused my order with a generous amount of his secret-special creamy pepper sauce and handed me the warm cardboard box with kindness. In all honesty, there have been times I took home an order of BangBang Shrimp and ate it with my fingers while navigating rush hour traffic. I longed to be full.

But now we had no more food anywhere in this part of the city.

So Josiah and I strolled together around the block. I jabbered away, about nothing in particular, asking him questions that he dutifully answered. I was honest with him.

"I don't know, Josiah, this year has been so hard. Sometimes I don't even know who I am anymore. I have a great support system, lots of help, I'm a grown up. I can only imagine how hard it's been for you kids."

He finally takes his mask off—the point of the Mask Break Walk is, after all, to get a break. I glance over at him quickly. He nods in agreement and we become equals, no longer student and teacher, just two human beings moving in tandem. That's it. I feel my heart needs to speak. "Sometimes I believe that the wind can blow all the bad feelings off me," and before I finish that sentence, the wind picks up with a cold, hard ferocity that actually moves us around in our steps. My impulsive declaration got such an eerie and immediate response that when I glance at his face again, he has the tiniest of smiles. I have never seen him smile. "Mr. Sea Glass! See? See? I had a lot of bad feelings that I needed to get rid of!"

We reach the straightaway along the parking lot and I now know he's OK with my talk. That to him, I'm sort of like a radio playing in the background, nothing for him to worry about. "You were the only one in your family until your little brother?"

He nods yes.

"Was it hard to be the only one for a long time then he came along?"

"It was hard," he admits.

"Yeah. I was the second child for a long time, then when I was five my little brother came."

I remember something that I want to tell Josiah. "When my little brother was two he had this little red car just big enough for him to sit in." I stop walking to act the whole thing out. Josiah turns to face me. "It had this enormous rubber band in the bottom, so I'd have to push and push it backward to wind it up. Then when it reached the end of being wound up—" I have stepped backward on the sidewalk pretending I am pushing the tiny car. "Then when I let it go, he'd go shooting down the street. He loved it."

It's as if my own little brother, laughing in his little convertible sports car, just went whooshing past us down the street toward the fire hydrant by the soup kitchen (empty now, no men getting hot meals since the pandemic began).

"My brother has a car," he says.

"Is it electric?"

He nods. We head back to the doors at the rear of the school. Past the broken window. The wind has stopped for a minute, and the sun warms us. I point to the decrepit building that sits outside our school, built during the Civil War, where the Colt Gun Factory used to store the ammunition. For ten years, I have walked around it, wondering what was inside. The windows are high up. Pigeons and sparrows live where the bricks have fallen out, and I try to pay attention to their songs every day when I pass this forlorn place heading into the school.

"I've looked at this building for ten years," I tell him. "Last week the doors were open! I have never seen that! I looked inside and it was so weird to see how—"

And for once, he actually interrupts me. "I saw that too!"

I expect him to tell me he saw what I saw: how creepy, how spooky.

"It's perfect for paintball."

I stop. "What?"

"Paintball."

I laugh and feel even more cleansed than when the wind blew on me. I have no idea how to play it, what the rules are; I never even knew you could do it inside. In my mind, I picture the cavern cleaned out, Josiah running with a paintball gun spraying pellets the sapphire-blue of his do-rag. I see him with other kids, roaring and running. I hear the laughing cries of a childhood before it went silent. I imagine his body as a boy before he became an old man. I think of who he was before he was broken. Before he turned into glass.

Kierique

She refused to come sit with us at the long rectangular science tables I put together in an effort to create a feeling of family being together around a dining room table. I covered them with hippie-tapestries for tablecloths and dotted the center with LED tealight candles that my kids with ADHD always played with like fidget spinners. Instead she sat at the one computer in the classroom, scrolling through photos of IHOP pancakes.

Who knew that there were thousands of images of pancakes on the internet? Covered in coned spirals of whipped cream, bejeweled with sliced strawberries and glistening with ruby syrup. Sometimes she'd switch to hundreds of photos of fried chicken.

She kept her eyes pinned to the screen, her long legs drawn up into the computer chair, her right hand on the mouse and her left hand holding tight to the metal desk, she swiveled the chair back and forth, never still.

She listened to everything going on in our discussion. When I'd call out her name to redirect her—"Kierique?"—to see if she was focusing, she would repeat back, verbatim, what had been transpiring in the class. For instance, "You said that Rayshawn made a good point about Langston, and then Carly said she thought the mom gave good advice about how to be strong." She whirled around to face me triumphantly. I'd laugh at her perfect summary, and her casual connection to using only Langston Hughes' first name. Langston.

I always use objects from nature as inspiration in the classroom: airborne milkweed, velvety leaves of wild Lamb's Ear. She wrote from the point of view of a bird's nest. "No one wants me, I'm left here, made of bits of mud and broken twigs, I fall apart in the wind." She had been through so much, so young. At nine, her mother had been sent to Niantic prison and Kierique had been left with an older cousin who, though a deacon in her church, beat her. When her mother was released when Kierique was twelve, they had not been able to reconnect emotionally. Her mother withheld food as a way to discipline her, and DCF got involved when Kierique would walk a mile on the highway for Flamin' Hot Cheetos at the all-night bodega.

The years that I had her, she was defiant, needy, rageful, funny, cruel, exhausted, sweet, lost. And fierce.

The thing about Kierique is that her smile, when it appeared, was incredible. Big, bright teeth. I guess sometimes in our superficial world, we have had standards that your teeth can't be too big—whatever that even means. Kierique's smile was a beacon; her teeth were slightly oversized and straight and bold and filled her smiling face. She was beautiful with perfect teeth.

Kierique left our program to attend a high school where she could graduate with fewer credits than what we required. She would not have to repeat her junior year, so she made the practical, mature decision to put her ragged academic past behind. She didn't want to leave our school by then because of how much we all loved her. And the whole faculty, though frustrated by her sassy antics, loved her. She'd come to visit me after she transferred, complaining about the unflattering khaki pants of her dumb school uniform. I can't recall how the joke started, but I once promised her I'd get her fuzzy dice to hang from her mirror when she got her first car. I kept them in my cabinet, tucked in the back. The day she came to see me and I surprised her with the gift, she flashed her big grin and patted me on the head, still teasing me for how she towered over my petiteness. "You're so short, are you OK?"

At the close of her senior year, she popped into my classroom and handed me an envelope. She was only allotted five tickets to her graduation, she said. And wanted me to have one.

To the G.O.A.T.

From: Your favorite student

God blessed me by putting you in my life, now to pay it forward I'm putting you in my graduation. June 10, 6:00 p.m. @ learning corridor

On the bottom there were two stick figures of different sizes, with the caption, *sorry we're bald, (us holding hands)*—

I'm still not sure if I am the little child or the big adult.

Because when Sea Glass Children come into your life, they connect you with the broken one you once were. You remember.

High up in my seat in the theater, I held my breath as "Kierique Rosalie Diaz" was called and she emerged from the wings. It took me a moment to recognize who she was now. Her bouncy mahogany curls were straightened and dyed blonde with a wash of pale teal, and she shimmered in her baby-blue graduation gown. I shouted her name, and in that sweet spot where a proud teacher can act like a crazed auntie, I stood and clapped and clapped long past the moment she once again took her seat and the next graduate already gripped hands with the principal. After the ceremony, I pushed through the pearly balloons and found her on the upstairs mezzanine, balling her head off. The tears on her amber face and her enormous rhinestone hoop earrings caught the light. She sparkled, collapsing into my arms so hard we staggered and almost fell. I could barely understand her as she choked on her words. "I— can't. I just—I nev—can't believe it. I. Did. This."

We jostled our way through the crowd to her mother and sister at the bottom of the stairs. Though the wound was still healing, I knew it had been a couple of years since Kierique's hardest times with her. Ma was only five feet tall, like me, and as we embraced then pulled apart, she grabbed my wrist, squeezing it with thanks. Kierique was no longer crying, but posing with her tassel on the left swinging, flashing that diploma, holding it pressed to her heart. It all felt like a raucous cocktail party, and I had to lean in and overlap with her mother and ask her to repeat the words several times. Finally, I understood.

My ear buzzed with Ma's, "Do you want to come out with us to IHOP?"

I laughed. I couldn't believe it. I knew what was in the little box I had for Kierique. I considered going. But it was already late. And it felt like a necessary time for just her family to feast, to be together. "I would love to," I shouted, "But I have to work in the morning."

The family nodded in understanding. I handed Kierique her gift. "Open it" I pantomimed.

With those coral, inch-long fingernails, she peeled back the tape. I waited for her to lift the lid and see that $50 gift card for IHOP.

T.S.

He was so suspicious for several years. I remember at the end of his junior year telling him how much it meant to me that he trusted me a bit more.

"I just don't trust teachers, Miss," he confessed one day. "Don't take it personal. It's not you. You're actually doing good."

I teased him. "So, then, what grade would you give me?"

He hesitated for only a moment. "An 80."

"A solid B-. Thank you! I'll take it!"

But then, his senior year, we survived the pandemic together, and one day, he said I had earned an A. Everything changed. T.S. and I spent so many mornings together, and I cried when, a year following Kierique, he graduated, too. In the Year of School Silhouettes, he walked down the baseline at the outdoor Dunkin Donuts Stadium as his name was called, that familiar way he moved like a boxer headed toward a championship fight in the ring. There's a roll of his shoulders, not tense, but ready to dodge, or to strike. Alert. Not wasting any energy. And a bit of a figure-eight shoulder glide.

Of all the kids I taught over the years, I valued his respect the most because it took me the longest to earn it. He never shared much about his home life, but I knew enough to know that it was volatile, as mine as a teenager had also been. I, too, was silent about it. We each kept it remarkably, impressively hidden. In my heart I held the truth of our connection. We both knew that I was a mandated reporter, and he made sure I had no specifics, no details.

I thought my heart would shatter with fullness when he began to feed me. In the lonely, empty, masked, cautious, broken world of our school, he brought me Welch's Fruit Snacks from the cafeteria lunches. Many days, I had time alone in my classroom, doing paperwork for a few free minutes. And there would be a knock, and I would get up and open the door, and he would be standing there in his mask, handing me the tiny sack of treats.

I had never eaten them before that, and I began loving their gummy texture and citrusy tang. It got to the point where I'd wait for that knock on the door. And it always came. Every single day, this kid brought me part of his cafeteria lunch. "Are you sure?" I'd ask. And he said, "It's OK, Miss, take them."

In early April, two weeks after my second COVID-19 vaccination, we stood at my open door and I held my arms open for an embrace. He was the first student I hugged in a year—and my school was, in normal times, very demonstrative. We put our arms around each other. It was awkward and wonderful. As we let go, he said, "I like hugs," so simply and sweetly I wanted to cry. Because when an emotionally broken child can receive and acknowledge waves of love, it smoothes the serrated edges of the heart.

Mine.

T.S.'s poem, junior year, reflecting on who he once was:

I am 14, and made of silence,
feather pillows, and loneliness,
waiting for the next
worksheet and hearing
gossip
and talk of ball and hoops.
I am made of ear buds, and a 40
minute walk with

sore arms and a

backpack slung across my back.

I am a puppy

who needs

attention, who

needs friends to love and care for him,

to be spoken to like

a baby.

We're sea glass. Hold us all up to the moon and let the light shine through.

Solaray

On the coldest day of the school year in January, eight degrees, hardly any kids came to school, choosing to stay in their beds and "distance learn" through Zoom. That day, I had only three students: T.S., Andre, and a student named Solaray who wasn't even officially enrolled in my class; she just liked us and became one of us. I nicknamed her Little Ray of Sunshine, and not just because her name was a variation of the Spanish word for sun. Every morning she entered the room, pint-sized in her glamorous wigs and child-sized Crocs. I was genuinely glad to greet her, always impressed and oohing and ahhing over her stylish transformations.

Sometimes Solaray's hair was lustrous as Princess Jasmine, swinging long and straight down her back; other times she sported a chic, geometric bob, or a halo of springy black curls, or a mod, high, Dream-of-Jeannie ponytail. Occasionally she wore no wig, just her own very short hair slicked down with edges and pin curls spiraled along her cheeks like a 1920s flapper. Her brown cheekbones glowed with a gossamer copper sheen, her eyelids often shimmered a peacock blue. I have no idea how she navigated through the halls; those fake eyelashes were so fringed and long. I worried about her physical vulnerability, slight and slim as a middle schooler, because I was pretty sure she wasn't going to grow much more at the age of nearly eighteen.

Solaray had no concern about how tiny she was. Because she knew she made up for it in sheer rhythmic fluidity. This girl could *dance*. Having taken lessons since she was three, she had recently achieved national recognition for her choreography that led to receiving a full dance scholarship to NYU. She could turn the most basic movements into visual poetry. That freezing morning she entered class and asked brightly, "Maureen, do you want to learn how to do a TikTok dance?"

Three kids. Masks. The utter despair of our COVID-19 school situation. I knew I'd have to force myself to be cheery when I opened up the Zoom class and no one showed their face or answered me when I said hello. I only knew that TikTok dances were when a few people stood together and matched movements like Motown backup singers in a band. Andre was eager to join us, and T.S. said he would film with my iPhone. "Sure. Why not?"

"OK, let's practice. Follow along with me."

Solaray was an excellent teacher: patient, kind, and enthusiastic. I did everything I could to imitate her closely, but my moves were a very vague facsimile. She was so good. We were not allowed to show our students' faces on Instagram, so we had T.S. film our dance from the back.

That day Solaray was wearing teeny black-and-white checkered Vans in the center of our video. Her voice is heard, counting down, "5, 4, 3, 2, 1" and then T.S. laughs at how serious and poised we are. We all begin shaking our hips and rocking to the music, lift our right arms, index fingers pointed, then we cross our wrists repetitively and bend our arms up. The corresponding lyrics bounce, "la-dee da-dee dee, la-dee dah-dee dah, you call my name and I lose my brain" and we circle both hands near our ears like gesturing "cuckoo." You hear Solaray cry out, high-pitched, and Andre's joyous chuckle, and me laughing too. The song continues, "and I float up to the moon." Only twenty-five seconds, but a long enough dance to create pure connection between us, and delight within.

We got so many responses with exclamation points and fire emojis when we posted it on Instagram that we did another TikTok the next week. This one had a "dice roll" move where you quickly mime shaking dice, your wrist close to your body. But as I was learning it, I had a slow-motion exaggerated dice roll. Ridiculous and way off-beat. Solaray and Andre found this hilarious, the classroom echoing with Andre's contagious laugh. They were not laughing *at* me; they were simply enjoying my "teacher variation." I felt accepted for being an uncool dancer, just a woman breaking out with a fresh angle on a move. We filmed it with them on each side of me, and me strutting toward the camera as I rolled my "dice" in my fist.

The children's choreography taught me everything I ever need to know about the healing magic of being silly together. If I shared here, beyond even the burden of the pandemic, what these two had survived, you wouldn't believe they could transcend it. I'm telling you though, sometimes they did. These kids had inconceivable losses considered the most difficult thing any human could survive. They were at times curled up under the desks unable to cope. They were at times dancing.

Dove Bars

If I could speak directly to the miracle of the loaves and fishes, and tell it how much it's sustained me over this last decade, I'd cry and tell it, *You hold such beauty for me.*

This miracle entered my life when I myself had been gutted like a fish and I understood nothing. I had been gutted like a fish, and there's no other way to describe it. Well, perhaps there is, but I don't want to. I always use that phrase; I won't change it. I also always say, "crash landed" when I describe how I began the Franciscan way.

Years back, in the months following my cancer diagnosis, I was a mess. Of course, my "mind" doesn't remember the surgery, but my body does—and did. Exhausted, because they had cut me open to cut out part of my intestines, cut the cancer out, sewed me back up, but first, in order to do that, they had pulled my intestines from my body. Then they stuffed them back in. The emotional and physical pain of the winter that followed was immense. My doctor strictly instructed that I could only eat the simplest food. Grits, instant mashed potatoes, Wonder Bread, and more grits. For over a month, that white, white food was all I could tolerate, so soft, as it slid along the stitches within my new body. This is the truth of both the cancer and the after-cancer body; it's very personal.

What is also personal is how this shifted my experience of communion into what I would call a "committed relationship." I had gone back into the classroom to teach, but I'm still not sure why I returned to work so soon when I couldn't even wear pants with zippers; I could only pull on loose black sweatpants over my pajama bottoms. The reality of cancer being found within me filled me with a terror I had never known before. This is why I found a church close by my school that had noon Mass. Once again, just like my addiction, I was given the gift of desperation. And that's how I ended up at St. Patrick–St. Anthony, huddled in the corner of the wooden pew that allowed me to lean, because I could barely sit upright.

As I curled around myself, I became enraptured with how one of the priests, Father Cid, held the Eucharist aloft. I'd never seen anything like this; he'd gaze at with such an adoring expression of love that I almost felt compelled to look away, because it was so intimate. When I received communion from him, he lifted the wafer up from the chalice, said, "Body of Christ," and then his hand floated down as if gliding through water as he placed it, pearly yet dry, into my cupped, empty hands. I ate it and blessed myself and, after swallowing, envisioned the light of Christ touching the dark world within, the broken-open and reattached places within me. I told no one I pictured this noontime communion as a firefly blinking through my sewn-together pieces, because I was afraid of being judged as ludicrous. I do not fear that now.

The way Father Cid flowed within Mass was a sacred body language all its own. Alongside this, though, was the fact that his Creole accent could be difficult to decipher. I understood "Je-sus Christ," but there were many homilies I could barely follow. He was aware that his accent was thick as he was learning to speak

English, so he'd enunciate very carefully into the mic, then pause while his deep voice still reverberated high in the cathedral ceiling. I'd catch random words, sometimes decrypting fuller phrases.

And then came the day I thought he had reached the end of his homily. With Father Cid, the long pauses were easy to confuse for closure. "Oh yes," he smiled, and pointed up, "God gives us (words I did not understand). He al-so gives us (a word I did not understand)." Then he folded his hands together over his robe and stood, head slightly bowed, his eyes blinking several times, reflecting. But he wasn't done. He opened his arms wide. And for the first time, I got the entire sentence.

"Take your lit-tle fi-shes and your loaves to the Lord, and see the miracle of what he can do." He took a deep inhale, long exhale, turned, and walked back across the sanctuary.

The gift of being broken open is that beautiful words enter your body through those empty spaces. Through that hunger to be, once again, somehow whole. That perfectly spoken sentence resounded like a bell. Like Thich Nhat Hanh's bell: When you hear the sound of it, you return to yourself. You come home.

I can't continue to talk about another gift from Father Cid without going back into even more pain. I cannot, at this writing, bear the burden of going back. Much of what I've written about that time I've chosen to not publish. It's funny, working in memoir, people think a goal is to "tell all" about what happened, and many memoirists do. For me, it's not about "what happened" but "how did it teach me, transform me?" I take the suggestion from Twelve-Step programs, to "look at the past, but don't stare." Staring risks the disorientation of tripping and falling into the destruction and its aftermath. Looking back is perhaps just throwing a pebble onto the surface of memory and seeing that you are sometimes still encircled by the widening rings of grief.

And so I will share the story of another phrase Father Cid gave me, not at the time it happened, but showing how it's become a part of me. This past year, I've been sent on a fresh path, publishing a book on how the psalms got me through very difficult times. The book had led me to connections in new places. During my second author visit to St. Francis of Assisi Church in NYC, I ended up afterward in a sun-filled dining room eating lunch with the priests. I had never had lunch with priests before. At the table with Father Tom and Steve (another priest), I was talking about how, in my view, priests are conduits.

"You never know what you say that people might hang on to," Steve admitted.

Father Tom emphatically agreed. "And sometimes you don't even remember saying the words! And later people will come to you and tell you how much the words meant."

"That happened with Father Cid," I said. "Do you remember that storm from ten years ago?" Father Tom had been head of St. Patrick's in Hartford for a long time, before being transferred to New York. He nodded, "Oh my gosh, yes."

I will look back for a moment, to October 2011: snow, sleet, and freezing rain fell for days in long slants like razor blades tearing everything open. Hundred-year-old trees came crashing down and actually shattered, tangling the power lines that then snapped. Live wires snaked across the sidewalks; roads became impassable; we were declared a disaster. The sun eventually returned, and the whole world churned with chainsaws in the round-the-clock cleanup.

There was unbearable destruction in my life then; in the year of my cancer, my marriage died—but I will not stare.

"Well," I continued, "when all of you stood outside on the sidewalk after Mass, I greeted Father Cid. We had been without electricity, no power, for more than a week."

"It was unbelievable." Father Tom's eyes widened in memory.

"So I was simply making conversation with Father Cid, and I said, 'I just got my power back after eight days.' And I mean, there had been hundreds of thousands of us without power, right? All over the Northeast. Such a mess. And he pulled his hand from mine, and—" here, I did my best impression of Father Cid. I shook my fists in celebration, threw back my head, eyes looking heavenward and sang out, "'Imagine the joy you can have!'"

Father Tom and Steve burst out laughing at my spot-on Father Cid impersonation. Making people laugh always energizes me.

"What an amazing thing to say!" I gushed. "I never forgot it. Here I was, just talking about something as simple as electricity, and he's ecstatic. And there I was wondering why he would have that severe reaction, and it was like, uh, Maureen, this guy's from *Haiti*, he's walked through the rubble of the earthquake. So yeah, maybe really let go and be fully alive in appreciation of the electrical power! Maybe don't take the most basic things for granted! Not just with gratitude, but *joy*. Those—" I counted them out on my fingers—"six words have never left me."

I was moved by the beginning of friendships here, the hospitality of these men. At the table next to us, other priests were quietly eating. I had spent the hours before lunch reading to this friar community from my book, basically pouring my heart out, and everyone had been very polite, thanking me. Because no one said much else, I was concerned I had not impacted them. But as we ate together, one of the priests from the audience turned to me, his spoon held aloft and asked, "Have you ever heard the Rufus Wainwright version of *Hallelujah?*"

I hesitated. So they had been listening when I read! Out of all the topics I covered—despair, loss, hope, renewal—he was asking me about the paragraph in my chapter on the psalms of David, where I mentioned that kd lang sang my favorite version of the Leonard Cohen song. "No," I answered.

Another priest at his table joined in. "Yes, I think you'd like the Rufus Wainwright version."

The conversation, light and simple. I loved it. Can't joy be soft and simple? Can't it just be the delight of eating lunch together? That meal? One of the best grilled cheese sandwiches ever, with the thickest bread and gooiest cheese. The tomato soup was home-made, speckled with basil, ladled by Father Tom into my bowl from a steaming urn. A homey, comfort-food feast, complete with fruit salad crowned with enormous shiny blackberries. They all had been so generous with their time inviting me up to lunch with them. I didn't want to leave this haven, but I didn't want to be a burden. I began to tuck the books they had kindly given me into my backpack.

"Would you like some ice cream?" Steve asked as we pushed in our chairs and cleared our dishes.

Father Tom teased me, "You told me earlier how you are trying in your life to receive all the good. That you are trying to 'say yes.'" His bald head glowed golden in the kitchen light.

I turned to Steve, who'd already plucked us both two mini Dove Bars from their freezer and handed me one. "They're only 100 calories," he joked as we each tore off our wrappers to reveal the chocolate coating. Our eyes widened in delight as we bit in.

In late 2020 I had not known that in the swirl of reassignments shifting all the friars around, Father Cid would disappear to the St. Anthony Shrine in Boston. It seemed I had him as a guide for such a short while, but that's not accurate. It was nearly ten years. I just grow spiritually at the same rate it takes to learn to fluently speak a language. By the time Father Cid left, his English was so smooth, I understood almost every single word he said.

I'm grateful that I'm in a place in my life where I offer a spontaneous "thank you" to someone out of the love in my heart, and not just when facing the loss of them under duress. The last time I saw him, before knowing he was leaving, I stopped him in the center aisle after Mass.

"Thank you for all you do." I held back tears.

"What is it I do?" He was genuinely curious, baffled even. He took my hand and sandwiched it in the warmth of his two palms.

"You have a very, very, very, very deep faith." With each "very" I felt I was entering something deeper. I actually would have kept going infinitely with the "verys," but I didn't want to take up too much of his time.

"It was a gift," he replied. "And you have it too, inside you. Thank you."

His belief in what I carried was so unshakable that I felt completely unhinged and vulnerable. Opening his arms at the same pace he raises and lowers communion, he embraced me delicately, his robe like the silken wings of a bird. I was filled up with love. He's gone now, out there serving at the shrine somewhere in Boston. I gather what he left behind.

The Periphery of Your Sigh

I understand that perhaps I qualify as a "religious weirdo" or, more accurately, in the words of Francis, I'm a holy fool. As I write, a familiar instrumental jazz song swings on WWUH and it takes me a bit to recognize what it is; it's the old Doobie Brothers song from 1979, one of the most devastating years of my former blackout life: "What a Fool Believes."

I am still reluctant, ambivalent, in sharing how I love looking right at Jesus. The change is within me: I can no longer keep him on the periphery of my sigh. I meant to tap out: keep him on the periphery of my *sight*. How I love this possibility of him being there, too, on the edge of my sighing.

I live in a world of typos. Recently I crossed paths with an image of a twelfth-century fresco in Austria, and when writing about Jesus taking that first loaf, I claimed the child "still held four loves in his arms." Four Loves. All the mistakes that I make, all the mix-ups, the missteps, still leading me, perhaps, into the loaves, beyond sighing.

• • •

Whoever he is, he's ineffable and boundless. Or so it seems to me. When I'm scared of putting my faith out into the world, when I hear myself lament, "I never wanted to end up this way," what I'm saying is that I never planned on writing the truth of how I've always needed to find his face, to turn it toward me. The Sacred Heart I keep near my bed sees me with eyes of love, acceptance, tenderness, hope, grounding. I always will have a hungry part, that baby I once was, arms reaching up. In the decades I've lived since being in a crib, the decades since carrying babies of my own, my need has only gotten deeper. The more heartache I've suffered and the more suffering I've witnessed, what I need most is someone—a brother, Jesus; a mother, Mary—who will never leave me.

No matter how or why it's happened, these three words, *gather the fragments,* elicit within me a desire to protect them, the surest sign of love. Fragments have a bad reputation that they're less than, incomplete, surpassed. But bread is both whole and made to be broken open, honoring the parts of us sullied and hurt, with a center of untouched purity that has never known disappointment or violence or betrayal.

• • •

I am driving down the road toward my favorite walking site. It's humid, but nothing like it was yesterday. I'm overwhelmed. I can't even finish reading any articles right now. International news, social issues, issues of faith. Just as one violent or tumultuous news story recedes, the next one appears. I live in a scorched world. What can I bring? I try to be true in who I am, clear in my refusal to give in to cynicism. I don't talk of Christ, though, not outside of church. I code-switch all the time. I offer freely, in many conversations, "I have a very deep faith," but I don't often mention Jesus. I keep him as a hidden indwelling, like my heartbeat; he's there, soft—can anyone hear it?

The fragments of love are not lost, scattered things, but are within me as I drive the S-shaped road I've driven down hundreds of times before. The miracle speaks into the scarcity in me, reaching at last to the place of enough. Why didn't he create just exactly what everyone in the crowd that day needed? Certainly he could have. Why was there extra, so much?

I think the unequivocal answer is: he never measures and weighs, doesn't count, keep score, or tally what is given. He just gives. A feeling wells up and overtakes me: *He just wants to feed all of us.* And before I know it, I'm crying, envisioning the people around the world with our divisions disappearing. Billions and billions of us with no labels, no names, no groups, no separations. Just all of us, human beings, calling out together on this planet. Can you hear our canticle?

Bread Ode

For fourteen thousand years, since the first charred breadcrumbs, we've hungered for it all over the globe. We roll it, wrap it, brush it with egg wash, dry it in the sun. We stuff it with sweet, meaty walnuts, orange zest, vanilla, or cheese. We slide it into wood ovens and slip it on griddles and fry pans. Close our eyes and inhale the kitchen scents of cardamom and saffron.

We shape *Naan* into teardrops. *Nan-e Sangak* into little stones. *Vanocka* to look like Jesus in the manger. *Tsoureki*, into three braided strands for the Trinity. *Pane Carasau*, *carta musica*, parchment of old music sheets. *Pan de Muerto*, layered on top, we devour the bones of melted cinnamon and anise.

Pasca, we share the loaves resembling the sun. *Pan dulce*, in shapes of *conchas* and *canastas*: we offer one another warm sweetened seashells and baskets.

Pao de Deus, bread of God.

A map of our continents pinpoint the hot cross buns, pita, frybread, soda bread, tortillas, cornbread, bagels, scones. Crumpets and banana bread, *roosterkoek, roti canai*. Untying the polka-dotted wrapper of Wonder Bread. Waiting for our supper and rushing to the table so famished we tear apart pairs of our *ciabatta*-slippers.

The Breaking

Turbulence

It's the word no one wants to hear while 30,000 feet in the air. And so, when, on United Airlines Flight 309 flying to Atlanta we all abruptly freefall and drop down, feeling it first in our guts, a scooping, it's terrifying.

What always strikes me about *turbulence* is suddenly being near strangers who are frightened. It's intimate. I think of fear as being a personal and private thing that you keep hidden inside when in public. But we're packed tightly into our seats in the clouds, and, as the pilot warns us to put on our seatbelts, the pitching worsens. I hear cries of passengers I cannot see, the sharp "Ohh!" sounds of women as a baby close to the wing begins a high-pitched wail. We bounce and dip to one side, then the other. The noise of the plane is deafening.

The woman next to me begins to pray. Over the din of the plane shaking and bucking, she begs, "Jesus Christ, I..." That's all I hear. We're all wearing masks and words disappear. I'm not sure exactly what she's asking for, but I can guess; she's squeezing the armrests, her eyes are closed tight, all alone with God in the sky. Our arms are brushing but I don't know what to offer. She can't hear me. All I know is she has a perfumed glamour, manicured fingernails, and fancy jeweled rings on fingers of both hands. From the way she pronounces "Jesus Christ, in your name, I..." I think she might be Jamaican, and then she's drowned out again.

We glide, smooth for a minute as everyone takes a breath and then we fall again and rise, fall and rise. I cry out too, against my will. Alone on this trip, I'm far from my daughter, completely cut off. My son doesn't know his mother is so afraid. I turn to the man on the other side of the aisle one row behind me. I cannot see above his blue mask; I can only see that his eyes, within his brown skin, are incredible anchors. He's also scared, looking right into me. I don't need to see his whole face because his expression conveys everything. Saying, "Hold on." We lock eyes for quite a while. I nod, trying to convey that I understand he's assuring me I'm not alone. The plane continues moving up and down. My stomach flip-flops. The man lifts his hand, makes a fist. I know what this means: *be strong, you got this.* I raise my fist in answer, *I will be strong.*

We pass through the turbulence at last and fly smooth, everyone subdued, drained, as we descend. Our wheels touch with a collective smattering of applause that we're safe and whole on our earth again. As the overhead compartments all click open and everyone scrambles for their bags, I turn to him. "Thank you so much for your kindness."

He nods. "I'm just glad everyone is OK."

We deplane, and he pulls his bag behind him. The bent angles of his long legs blend into the overflowing crowd of the terminal. Though he becomes a helper I will never see again, I can feel how the watermark of his kindness will last.

I have a two-hour layover, and few seats are open except along the food court. Settling in with my carry-on bag on my lap, I watch the unbroken procession of people. It's been over a year, close to a year-and-a-half, since I encountered so many people, and I'm fascinated by how ordinary everyone is. Since the pandemic began, the fear has been nonstop: Someone could infect me. I could infect them. We still live with that. But we're all lost birds now, trying to fly to the missing members of our flock, the faraway ones we love. No matter the gender, age, race, or identity, we are all dressed in cotton shirts with sports teams or uplifting messages, jeans, and sneakers. Wearing our masks and holding our coffee cups. No matter where we live, or where we are from, none of us is home.

I distractedly scroll on my phone and open an email from my church. There's a link to today's Mass, so I click it. With no headphones, I press the phone close to my ear to listen to Father Bill's homily. It's the reading of the Loaves and Fishes. Father Bill is new to our parish, and I've flagged his homilies as awesome. He's very articulate, funny, and at times, unyieldingly serious. He's a real wordsmith. I love it.

I feel incredibly alive somehow, listening to his words about my favorite miracle as the couples and families form lines to order soft pretzels, sandwiches, and muffins. Father Bill is talking about our obligation to the poor, our part in the miracle. He's saying something about Jesus pushing back. I hear Father Bill, with a tone in his voice, "*You* feed them." Then it cuts off.

What a disappointment to have the homily unfinished! I rewind it a bit to catch the ending, and watch it now too, his face on my screen, his gray and brown beard, his eyes growing stern as I listen again to what he said, "*You* feed them." The recessed lighting shines directly above and covers his shaved head with white-light spangles. His challenging gaze sweeps across the audience, then he turns. That *is* the last line.

Jesus asked how many loaves they had, and first put the onus on us. We have to be here for one another with helpings of love and understanding. With mercy, patience, kindness. I am dumb-founded by how true this is. How earlier that day in the sky, alone in the gust loads and wind shears, the man on the plane witnessed my anguish, and with hope and strength, he fed me.

The Big Dipper

In the mystical moist night-air, and from time to time, / Look'd up in perfect silence at the stars. —Walt Whitman

I call my parish "the sacred oasis at the edge of the city." I go for spiritual sustenance, but others go for the two slices of meat within two slices of bread, handed out seven days a week at the north side of the church, the Sandwich Door. On Tuesdays and Thursdays, there are hot meals, and student nurses from St. Joseph College offering to check blood pressure and sugar levels of, as the church calls them, "our guests." Throughout the six months of winter, pairs of socks and gloves are also distributed.

When I watched Father Bill's Loaves and Fishes homily on my iPhone in the Washington, DC, airport, his last line reverberated: "*You* feed them." Recently I asked him for a copy; all his homilies are useful, pitched with precision. But when I read it, I realized I was definitely benefiting from a do-over in seeing the intent of what he was saying. Had I understood him at all?

He writes of the story:

No doubt, it was preserved and retold by several different communities in the early church, partly because it was so spectacular and partly because of its eucharistic overtones, a dimension we will hear for several weeks in the Sunday Gospels. So we will have ample opportunity to reflect on the gift of the Eucharist in our own lives. But this weekend, it is food for the body not food for the soul I wish to highlight. Because like that crowd on the Galilean hillside, our world is physically hungry. Some 700 million people experience chronic hunger; 30 percent of the world's children are severely undernourished; 45 percent of deaths of those under the age of five are hunger related. It isn't as if there's not enough food to go around...our fields, orchards, feedlots, barnyards, silos, and warehouses are chock full of fruits and vegetables, meats and sweets, protein, fats and carbs of every kind. But abundance, like scarcity, is unevenly distributed, and vast numbers of our brothers and sisters, both at home and abroad, have little or no access to the table of plenty.

The disciples said to him, "This is a deserted place and the hour is now very late; send the crowd away so that they can go into the surrounding villages and buy something for themselves to eat." But Jesus answers them by saying: "You give them something to eat."

When I first heard how emphatically Father Bill spoke that line, I thought it tingled with outrage. But in reflecting, it's more like protection, if protection could be an emotion. Isn't it?

Those who spend hours of their lives trying to feed the hungry are often frustrated by the bottomless well of need. But if a speckled star hung upon each entrance in this city offering food, the surface of that well would undulate with flickering light, a Big and Little Dipper, a constellation. Because in Hartford, a city with a childhood poverty rate of 30.5 percent, in spite of divisions and oppositions among faiths, denominations, and beliefs, the faithful are heeding the words "you feed them." The starlight would lead us through the windy corridors of blowing cinders to sunrise, breakfast at the Greater Refuge Church of Christ, or the Walk of Light Outreach Center, or Shiloh Baptist. Then the points could guide us to lunch at MANNA Community Meals, House of Bread, Loaves and Fishes on Woodland Street, St. Monica's Episcopal, or back to the heart of the city at Christ Church Cathedral. Yes, different Christian perspectives—Three Angels Baptist Church, Our Lady of Sorrows—but all with hands dipping ladles into industrial-sized stockpots and pouring the next bowls of today's soup.

Evening comes with the first star and a crescent moon over the knot of the intersecting highways, and the hungry seek a sandwich. They cross the darkening concrete and cement. They knock. Someone opens and greets them with a cookie and a juice box. And a sandwich with the peanut butter and jelly spreading to reach each of the four sides, all the way to every corner of the bread.

Angel Beanie

Lemon drops

She is weakened and scared, strong and brave. She's getting chemo and radiation at the same time, and I want to drop off lemonade and lemon drops because I read online it can counter the metallic taste in her mouth from the chemo. Angelica is the model of equanimity, no self-pity, no rage. Each day she drives herself two towns over to radiation after teaching twenty-eight preschoolers all day.

I want to take care of her. I wish I could fix her. I'll bring her favorite soup, chicken noodle and mushroom, and fresh-squeezed lemonade. Even though she said, "Don't bother. I'm not hungry." Her brother has COVID-19 in the ICU in California. In spite of all her heartache, I'm glad she wants to see me.

Angelica is Colombian with ebony curls on her head. We both wonder, will these spirals disappear as she continues with her treatments? It seems forever since we worked in classrooms that connected and we could see one another simply by knocking and then opening the door. We laughed a lot communicating that way, because we were always confused about some spontaneous, cockamamie directive from administration. Together, we'd figure out what we were being asked to do. Miss Anita was on the other side of me, but with no connecting door, so I'd have to scurry down the hallway quickly—with those walls of windows facing the geometric Hartford skyline—to speak with her. All three of us bonded as artists, then as friends.

Now years later, we try our best to keep up with one another, to meet. When I call Anita, she asks, "Have you talked with Angelica? What's going on?" And I share the news. Angelica always asks, "Hey, so have you seen Anita?" I did see Anita, in her red kayak on the Farmington River. We talked despondently about Angelica's diagnosis, our love for her and our concern, and nothing else could be said. Anita held still from paddling for so long all the waterdrops stopped falling from her oar and she let the river and her sorrow just take her.

Entering the Exit

Angelica's brother died of COVID yesterday. She has taken a leave of absence from her job to still go to radiation and chemo every day. I'm beyond sad for her. Beyond sad for her mother, who accompanies Angelica now to her appointments. Her mother is still grieving the loss of her husband two years ago, now grieving the loss of her son while her daughter undergoes treatment for a rare and aggressive cancer.

I dreamt of Angelica. In my dream, I heard her lament, her sorrow, her voice. All I could understand was her repeating, "I can't," with other words I could not decipher. It was a vulnerable, out-of-control cry. Her most hidden private grief coming forth from her center.

I am powerless, and once again I hate it. I hate seeing a person knocked over and knocked down by so much pain and loss. I don't understand God. When she was telling me her brother died, I was driving home. I pulled into St. Anne's Cemetery, going the wrong route, entering at the exit. Surrounded by the hillside of well-tended, recently arrived gravestones, she told me, on speakerphone, that she heard and saw her brother's last breath on a FaceTime call. Her voice was so soft and broken. After she hung up, I drove home imagining what it would be like to see my brother die that way. I would be devastated.

Beanie

We are sitting in Angelica's car and have been talking for an hour in the late afternoon darkness. She drove all the way from Manchester, over the mountain to come get me when I told her I was feeling painfully sad. I did not want her to come. She is the one who needs the extra love! But she disagreed and drove in rush hour traffic to my house and took me to Whole Foods.

It's a front-seat-of-the-car moment. It feels holy. Sharing face-to-face is much richer than the phone, although if all we can usually have in our busy lives is our hour-long calls, that's OK; it's the way it is. But what a relief to share our stories of the hardships of our families. Conflicts, misunderstandings, resentments, all the things we cannot undo; we must accept them as they are today. "I'm hungry, are you? Let's go." Her little hat. You know you really love your friend when you love how cute they look with the drape of their wool beanie, that loose part that bends at the top, how it's empty.

We enter Whole Foods and spend a long time wandering around and around the Hot Bar, discussing all the possible selections for our dinner. There's so much to choose from, plus the long, cold aisle of colorful, fizzy canned drinks and glowing glass bottles. She forces me to get some fresh-baked cookies and demands that I also allow her to buy a wax bag of black-and-white cookies for me to take home to my son. Into her basket she drops a few round disks, a Korean frozen dessert, which I've never had and don't quite understand what it is. They're called "Bubbies."

The fun of perching on high stools at the counter eating Spicy Jamaican chicken and jasmine rice, to be out together, our masks in our pockets for the meal. She's getting me caught up on her next cancer treatments, how it's going, what her doctors have recently said. We unwrap the disks and I take a bite, finding the pink center to be sweet, oozing, cold, and we laugh at how strange the dessert is, how delicious. Mine is mango. Hers is blood orange. We toss our cardboard containers into the trash and she drives me home. Getting out of the car, I joke, "Thanks for the Wellness Check."

She laughs, and I continue with the silliness. But I also mean it: "Need help? Call Angelica's Mobile Crisis. Call 211." The "I love you's" we say to each other overlap. I slam the door. She heads home and in the beam of the streetlight, the last thing I see is the familiar profile of her face and the bent silhouette of her beanie.

10,000 Sunflowers

Thich Nhat Hanh died in January 2022 at the age of ninety-five, teaching us lessons about peace and acceptance up to his last breath, and beyond. This monk, fluent in seven languages, spent the final seven years of his life wordless, as a catastrophic stroke in 2014 had rendered him unable to speak. Not a single word from this Zen master who wrote more than one hundred books, many bestsellers, translated into forty languages and read by millions all over the world.

Peace Is Every Step. Two Treasures. Peace Is Every Breath.

Somehow, he did communicate that he longed to return home to Vietnam. And so, no longer exiled, he lived the last three years within Root Temple. His decline and impairment are the things people are most terrified of. Many would proclaim how horrifying his ending was; they'd never want to find themselves like that. I've heard my friends say they'd rather choose their death than grow incapacitated and old. "Send me out on the ice flow." And other more violent or drug-fueled suggestions.

What Thich Nhat Hanh modeled was how to breathe peace in and out, to accept the full cycle of life unabashedly all the way to the end. The monks who ministered to him in his wheelchair—the familiar magnets of his pitch-black eyes and orb of his bald head tucked inside the brown monk's hood—shared that just being near him, they basked in peace and calm. Joy still burnished even from his withering.

When someone of his stature passes, the media reflects and honors and praises for a brief time, until the slate of obituaries, like the cremated ashes themselves, blow away. But true to his teachings, he lives on in how he transformed the world by bringing the idea of mindfulness to the West. His reach as a Buddhist, spanning decades, is unfathomable in its scope.

Two of his books live within me now, each having come to me at a certain phase of my life. The first and more recent, *Going Home: Jesus and Buddha as Brothers*, has a five-paragraph passage on love and suffering that I taught my rowdiest classes on Friday afternoons. By the end of the week my students had a receptivity, born of exhaustion, to philosophical ideas. Because my students lived weighed down by relentless suffering, I often sought counsel from my own teacher, Alice, about the nature of my curriculum. "Your students are old souls," she guided me. "They can understand in ways most adults can't."

When I'd read this section out loud, a palpable sense of comfort entered the classroom. Reading this passage again, now, I feel the relief of ceasing to beat my wings so hard, trying to escape. He writes:

> I would not be willing to go to a place where there is no suffering because I know that living in such a place I would not experience love. Because I suffer, I need love. Because you suffer, you need love. Because we suffer, we know that we have to offer each other love.[2]

I've lived my whole life trying to figure out how to outmaneuver suffering; yes, how to fly away. But I have no wings. What if I just surrender to his idea and let my suffering open to its fullest feathers of love? Both as a mother and as a daughter whose mother is now getting so old.

My daughter and I are talking about my mom, her grandmother.

"Grandma stays up till midnight coloring. It's true her memory is not great. I mean, it's old age. She'll ask the same thing over and over. But she's happy." My mother is still mobile, but no longer drives. Because of her worsening dementia, she requires 24/7 care. "Look at Thich Nhat Hanh."

"Yeah, I heard he died."

"I love Thich Nhat Hanh. He really helped me when you guys were little."

I think of the passage of time, the impermanence of our lives. I was once a young mother, as my mother was once a young mother. What became of the women we were? So long ago, I'd insert one of his tapes in my boom box on my dresser and take a power nap atop the quilt with my toddler son near, pressing into me, before we had to wake and I'd pop Max in the stroller to rush up to the elementary school to get my daughter. The gentleness of Thich Nhat Hanh's voice lowered the decibels of my angst.

I send my heart along with the sound of this bell
May the hearers awaken from their forgetfulness
And transcend the path of anxiety and sorrow

I struggled with catastrophizing, hyper-focused on all the possible dangers awaiting my children—how could I keep them safe? Over twenty-five years later, I envision the square box-cover of those tapes, their technology now obsolete. On an Easter-purple background, one snow-white lotus opened up wide, with a golden stamen. The words *The Present Moment* were written in gold matching the center of the blossom. Those six tapes brought me back to myself, my breath, my life, again and again. They kept me grounded, able to delight in the heat of my son's breathing against my bare arm.

"I remember that!" she laughs.

I'm curious. "What do you remember?"

She giggles. "You used to get so mad because we used to laugh at him."

I know what she's talking about. No, they didn't make fun of him, exactly; they'd get silly over a line spoken by his spiritual partner, Sister True Emptiness. When I imitate how she said it, "I see 10,000 sunflowers waving at me," my daughter and I share a long laugh. It's such a resplendent line—parallel to Ralph Waldo Emerson's "The earth laughs in flowers"—and I've never driven by a lengthy row of sunflowers, planted along a rural straightaway, and not heard her voice in my head. Those sunflowers wave at me, laughing. Laughing. And always will.

"So," Mad continues, "you're saying just let Grandma keep coloring."

"Yep. That's it."

I'm thinking about the incredible example Thich Nhat Hanh gave us for how to ride into old age. My face is a different face now, wrinkled. Perhaps I have another decade or two. My mother is a widow who flinches in pain when using her cane, and it shocks me to see her hobbling. How is this my mom? Her dementia encroaches. She remembers so little. And yet, she still throws her head back and laughs just as she always has. I get solace from the words of Thich Nhat Hanh who, in talking about both Buddhism and Jesus, gave us the image of how bread represents the endless flow of life, how it holds the sun, the wheat, the dirt, the clouds, the whole sky.

"Did you get much snow?" She asks me cheerfully on a phone call from her home in Maine.

"Yes," I say, "Connecticut got around half a foot. How about you?"

"No, just a few flurries. You know how much I wanted a big storm. We just got flurries. Did you get much snow?"

"Yes," I whisper gently, "We did."

The Fullness

Crèche of Rain

Beneath four vertical bells, the crèche outside the church holds
Mary, Joseph, and Gabriel, their faces bathed in the green glow,
then the red, of the traffic light. The tradition is to not put the
Baby Jesus (more formally the Christ Child) in the manger until
Christmas Day, to symbolize we are waiting for him as each night
grows longer, and he is not here just yet.

It's after five o'clock Mass, and I glance down into the cradle
made of white marble, or perhaps it's porcelain. I'm dismayed that
the place where Jesus will come has become a pool filled with
water, like a fountain. And in it, a leaf, a single maple leaf, is
floating. Here we are, each of us a leaf, alone, fallen, in the clear,
cold rain. It's so simple.

I'm a bit melancholic about this image, as the next week on
Sunday when moving my shadow so as to not block the shafts of
streetlight, I peer into the cradle, expecting again to find the water,
and it's gone. The leaf is gone. Someone's tended to the rain, dried
it up, maybe with a towel to absorb all the water. Who is the anon-
ymous soul who got this outdoor manger ready?

I think of Thomas Merton's idea that there might be twenty
people who see the world clearly, and then he decides, maybe

there are one or two. Even though the collective fear is that the world is falling apart, in fact, these people are keeping that from coming true. No matter the number, where are they? What if they are near us? These free people, doing all sorts of things completely unnoticed, trying to make the world a better place, somehow holding it together. We'll never know who they are. They're silent bells hanging above us. They move unseen in the quietude of our streets.

When I Was Hungry

Ringed in gold, they shine, the city wounds,
each the shape of a mandorla.

Ever since I began following the footsteps of Francis, I've been repeatedly led to places that, in unexpected ways, expand my ability to give and receive love. So when I was sent an invitation to do a book reading and signing at St. Francis of Assisi Church on West Thirty-First Street in New York City, I said yes right away.

My heart so full, knowing I was to be included in the parish of Father Mychal Judge. Now called the "Saint of 9/11" (he has a passionate following petitioning for him to become an actual saint), he was chaplain to all the New York City firefighters, and he's recorded as the first casualty in the World Trade Towers terrorist attacks. The photograph of his limp body being carried into the sunlight from the ashes is an iconic image, a pieta from one of the most violent mornings in American history. I discovered that in the AIDS epidemic of the late 1980s and early 1990s, Father Mike ministered to men of the gay community who were otherwise dying all alone, skeletal and scabbed, encircled in sores, rejected even by their own families. Here we are in 2022, and the church is still embroiled in issues surrounding the gay population. He wrote, *Is there so much love in the world that we can afford to discriminate against any kind of love?* I was honored to be invited to the church on Thirty-First Street, now renamed Father Mychal Judge Street, where they hold a Mass to welcome all before the annual New York City Gay Pride Parade. Because that's what followers of Francis do. They welcome all, seeing Christ in everyone.

I emerged from my train after a two-hour ride from Hartford, breathing in the stale, steaming underground air, then I climbed up the stairs into the glow of the Beaux-Arts magic of Grand Central Station. I delighted in the soaring, opulent architecture of Grand Central once again, the intricate chandeliers, and infamous brass clock in the center. It's always a bit scary for a moment, being enclosed in the rush and urgency of it all, but there's a thrill, too, that no other city can match.

It had been two years since I'd visited New York. As a woman who travels alone, my senses are always heightened. In particular, I listen. And I knew instantly the pandemic had irrevocably impacted the city. I heard it. I heard it in the voices as I joined the pedestrian crowd moving down Forty-Second Street. Every twenty feet or so a person cried out, in pain, in panic. Throngs of us flowing east and west on streets, and north and south on avenues. They cried out in fury with masks on their chins, they cried out in confusion, grimaces webbed with spittle.

And while it was still Manhattan, alive and moving with the breathtaking, kaleidoscopic variations of the human face, I was taken aback by the number of men in crusted windbreakers who urinated on the storefront scaffolding. Piles of green garbage bags, slung like sandbags to keep a flooding river from overflowing, rose at every intersection, and the sidewalks were a blur of spills and smears. The voices stamped in place alone on corners, in fervent conversation with phantoms floating around them, and I wondered if those phantoms also cried as they blew inside the wind, the wind that felt different now, torn apart with a palpable, ragged edge.

The city has always held infinite contrasts, and that day, though unnerved and saddened, I also felt deeply grateful and alive in the sixty-five-degree sun of that autumn afternoon. Since I live in forest dapple, I enjoyed dipping in and out of the angular shadows shaped by skyscrapers and fire escapes. I took a right onto West Thirty-First and I recognized the place of Father Mike's memorial, FDNY Engine 1, Ladder 24, across from the church spire with the tiled Francis flying high. It felt, oddly, like coming home. That was the way I'd felt in Italy at both La Cella and in Assisi, places where Francis loved and lived.

As I drew nearer, my eyes pinned to sculptured angels protecting, the scent hit me. The steps leading up to the church were saturated with urine drying in the sun. I had not expected this. I had never been to a church whose entrance smelled so horrible. I admit, at first it felt wrong. Not sacred. But that thought passed, thankfully. Because the opposite is true. Several homeless people crouched alongside the banisters with their bags. To the left of the church stairs a faceless human form slept under a soiled crocheted baby blanket.

Another human shape had permanently settled on the sidewalk. I realized this was a life-sized sculpture made of bronze. Sitting cross-legged, head hanging, face hidden, blanket concealing him, he extends his right hand out. Someone placed a russet-colored daisy in his open palm, and a stemless pink carnation in the folds of fabric over his heart. Every day hundreds of people—tourists, midtown workers headed to and from Penn Station's trains—pass this work of Timothy Schmalz, with the words on a wall sign that reads, "Whatsoever you do for one of my least brothers or sisters, you did for me—Matthew 25:40."

I climbed the pungent steps and a doorman opened the door to the inward beauty, or, to use a Franciscan word, I entered the indwelling. I snapped a number of photos and posted them on Instagram. One surprised me, striking a chord even with people who identify as non-religious. A carving of Mary with Asian children being protected under her robes (the church is in Koreatown). Above her, a more traditional Western art Blessed Mother is painted, surrounded by angels. It's a doublet, the same story repeated twice: A Mary protecting a Mary who's protecting.

The thing is, that night, I felt completely in love. Not with a person, and not only with the city, but with myself and with life. I was absolutely full. My loneliness, for the first time, no longer hurt me. I joined the crazy circus of a crowd in Times Square, gorging on the stimulation and the lights. I walked back to my hotel, passing the lions of the New York Public Library, treating myself to a sundae from one of the ice-cream trucks. It had been over a decade since I'd spooned whipped cream and hot fudge and ice cream, all three at once, into my mouth.

The next day, at lunch with Father Tom before my reading, he recounted that one of the homeless women who sat on the church steps told him how she was attacked one night.

"She was on the higher stairs, and a group of men came; they deliberately hurt the homeless. They pulled her hair and pulled her down the steps and beat her up."

Later, as we crossed the street together, the woman called out to me, "I like your dress!"

"Thank you," I called back, and her grin widened.

The reading allowed me to connect to people in a way that I never had before. Telling the truth about grace. About God. I felt so welcomed by the friars. *Hi, I'm Brian! Welcome, I'm Barry!* They had a lightness I can't quite pinpoint. They made me feel like I belonged there, no strings attached. Not because I had suffered and earned it, but because I was loved. And I was absolutely blown away when, unbeknownst to me, two of my students had trekked all the way to New York to support me. I cried when Gina and Kahron entered the San Damiano Hall.

When the event ended and I exited the church, the sculpture had changed. Someone left a clear plastic cup with a few sips remaining of a strawberry drink. Left behind either as a snide offering or as trash, it was disconcerting to view the fruity froth and the straw amid the sour wind. The pink carnation had slipped further down into his folds, now just peeking out. The other blossom was gone. I stepped closer to take a picture and saw a deep wound in the open outstretched hand.

Wait a minute.

This lost, faceless beggar has the gift of *stigmata?* Where the daisy had now blown away?

It's Christ on this city street.

Of course.

I heard the song in my head. *Whatsoever you do to the least of my brothers, that you do unto me.*

How did I not know this before?

But I didn't recognize it was him.

And what's even more illustrative of my inability to see, is that later, on the 9:23 train from Grand Central, as I looked back over all my photos, when the flower was in his palm, his wound was there all along, the edges ringed in gold. The blossom had not fully covered it. I simply did not take in the huge puncture, though I was looking right at it.

As I left that day, the homeless woman had been on the steps again, and she asked me for a dollar. I knew the church did not encourage direct giving, and so I did not give it to her. Her face fell in disappointment. What was her name? I had not remembered when Father Tom told me. I only knew her as the Homeless Woman. I began to suspect some lessons come to us twice for emphasis. And in the darkness of the train heading home, I saw I was wrong about the daisy blossom too. It had never blown away but remained, under his open hand, tucked there by the broken edges of the wind.

Take Your Bird Unto

Miracles cannot be contained. It's in their nature to climb one another, overlap and intertwine. One calls to me like a wild winter shrub, crimson in a monochromatic landscape, reaching skyward with delicate tapers. Then, as if it's a gray vine, another miracle rises from within the roots and wraps, spiraling upward around the red in a loose embrace. They grow together now, inseparable.

This is the simplest way I can outline the poetry of one sentence of dialogue from the Blind Man of Bethsaida. In Mark 8, things get a bit wild; three narrow columns of miracles spread as if with stolons, tubers, runners. The chapter opens with the second Feeding of the Multitude, this time, a crowd of four thousand. After this, Jesus left with the disciples in a boat, and when they become alarmed that they have no bread, he recounts; he reminds them:

> "Are your hearts hardened? Do you have eyes and not see, ears and not hear? And do you not remember, when I broke the five loaves for the five thousand, how many wicker baskets full of fragments you picked up?"
>
> They answered him, "Twelve."

"When I broke the seven loaves for the four thousand, how many full baskets of fragments did you pick up?"

They answered [him], "Seven."

He said to them, "Do you still not understand?"

When they arrived at Bethsaida, they brought to him a blind man and begged him to touch him. He took the blind man by the hand and led him outside the village. Putting spittle on his eyes he laid his hands on him and asked, "Do you see anything?"

Looking up he replied, "I see people looking like trees and walking."

Then he laid hands on his eyes a second time and he saw clearly; his sight was restored and he could see everything distinctly. (Mark 8:18-25)

I just love this. Halfway through the miracle, the blind man expresses himself clearly, yet it's a paradox because he's describing his confusion. Yes, it's what he sees, but it's not what's there. *I see people looking like trees and walking.* He's at the midpoint of understanding. The question for us is: how many times have we held onto a belief, or an opinion, not seeing clearly, yet claiming we knew the truth, certain of how it curved and blurred in the wind?

What about the many times my ears did not hear? During my overlapping cancer and divorce, the trials that led me to the healing of the psalms, I listened to a radio station that solely played original gospel-blues from the Black church. Admittedly, with the focus on recorded music from almost a hundred years ago, there weren't that many songs filling out the rotation. No matter: I waited for that tune to fly in, and to bring with it my two-and-a-half minutes of solace.

"Take your bird unto the Lord and leave it there, leave it there, take your bird unto the Lord and leave it there."

I envisioned cupping my little bird in my hands, trusting that God would take it as it hopped out of my palms into his. For months and months, I sang along before realizing I had the lyrics totally wrong. The words, one day, rearranged themselves. The correct refrain throughout is, "Take your burden to the Lord, and leave it there, leave it there, take your burden to the Lord and leave it there."

Burden. Not *bird unto.*

In defense of my blunder, the version was performed by the Sensational Nightingales, and one of the first lines declares, "Remember in his word / how he feeds the little bird." But I was wrong. When I learned the truth, I actually felt a sense of loss that I no longer had a bird to bring. This is a mild illustration of misinterpretation. My concern is the presence of larger, more damaging ones. Most alarmingly, the "truths" I've believed, leading me to see the people of the world askew, minimizing their value or worth, thus justifying my decision to push them beyond the orb of my care, or concern.

Mark 8 ends with the blind man receiving the second half of his miracle. Jesus touches him a second time, and he comes fully out of the darkness; thus now the blind man could see the people in his life. His village. His neighbors.

I don't want to draw conclusions that are based on half-blindness, as if the world is a stained glass window at night. Instead of a kaleidoscope of ruby and cobalt, with lambs a white glow, the stained glass at night makes me feel so uneasy. A horrible green cast, close to raw umber, hard to believe there's any story there, that it's anything other than puce fragments. The window is actually a pair, two arched halves, the whole surface wiggly lines. Without any sun shining through, the surface appears shattered with cracked lines in no pattern, a chaos making no sense.

Except.

Except on the upper right side, a shape becomes clear. The one thing that emerges in the empty disorder of the space is the sepia of Jesus' gaze under the circle of his halo. Even in the onset of dark hours ahead, in ugly mishmash, you can recognize his face. This miracle demands we keep going, climbing up. To let the vine of the miracle be full-blown. I want us to walk together, surrounded by real birds, by actual silhouettes of the trees. And mostly, I want to see you clearly in order to fully love you.

Turning Teal

At 11:30 a tall priest, one of the new ones who was transferred here last year and whose name I don't know, appears in the vestibule by the holy water fonts. Ever since March of 2020 the fonts at the entrance of the church have been dry, each covered over with an X of purple tape. I'm wondering if the watermarks near our hearts will ever return, even after the pandemic, or will we forever be entering and blessing ourselves with fingertips of air.

He glides past me down the side aisle. So it will be this guy. Not Father Bill, like I hoped. I don't know why I'm jumping in, but I've spent several seasons obsessing over which priest will be best for me, analyzing, over-thinking, procrastinating. Who is the best to choose so I get my well-deserved epiphany? Finally my inner critic had enough. Just go. Enough of this drama. Besides, it's not even called *confession* anymore. It has a new name: The Sacrament of Reconciliation. He disappears into the Reconciliation Room and shuts the door. Very quickly, a man pops out of the Chapel of Our Lady of Angels, and enters. So this is confession.

Soon it's my turn. I enter the room and am taken aback. It's not as I expected, all these months of projecting that it would be face-to-face. I thought that was the "new" way of doing it. But it's traditional, not an entire booth, but a wooden screen with the priest behind it. I lower myself onto the pleather of a kneeler that is unusually squishy; it lets out a long sigh as my knees sink. I am unsure what to say. Somewhere an official prayer exists about being contrite, but I never memorized it even as a child, so there's nothing I can try to remember.

"Good afternoon, Father."

"Good afternoon."

The lattice between us is garden-like, as if we're friendly neighbors greeting one another on either side.

"I haven't been here in a long time."

He waits.

I add, "A really long time."

There's no rush.

I just say it. "Thirty-two years."

I feel something here, a shift. As if we're being held within a sheltered ventricle together.

He laughs. "Well, welcome back."

I laugh and cry. "Thank you so much for that."

"It's not every day that I get to be part of this sort of return."

His genuine, joyful, spontaneous welcome of me is why I love the Franciscans. How do they do it, again and again, clear away all the rain and debris, finding love?

He asks, "Usually when someone comes back after that long, there's something taking place in their lives—is there something for you?"

"Yes. I come to Mass. I take communion. I want to do it right. I'm on a new precipice. I don't want a wedge between others and me, or between God and me. I want my side of the street to be clean."

"That's a lot of metaphors," he responds.

I laugh, and then we're laughing together. I'm a bit shocked at how closely he was listening.

"I'm a writer," I admit.

"I can tell."

The silence between us feels so refreshing.

"Why don't you pick one or two things you know you want to talk about?"

I name it. Envy. The vice that has dogged me my whole life, the character defect, fault, one of the seven deadly sins that has driven every Fourth Step of my sobriety. How it makes me petty, mean, self-pitying. The worst of it is how it clouds the brightness of my ability to open up to fully loving others. I feel uplifted just admitting it.

"Anything else you want to share here right now?"

"Yes. I have a hard time trusting in God sometimes. Even with all he's done. I get so afraid."

We're silent together again within the soft beating ventricle.

"I have a few ideas," he says. "Keep a gratitude list. Tomorrow write one thing. The next day, two. Then the next day, three things. Put it on your refrigerator."

Franciscans keep it real. You go to reconciliation for mercy, and they bring in the fridge magnets.

"The next idea is a gratitude photo. Each day take a photo of something you are grateful for. For a month. At the end of the month, it's an array of gratitude. As for the trust, have you seen *The Chosen*?"

"I've heard of it, but no."

"Try to watch it. It's really helped me see the human in Jesus, how to turn to him. For your penance, do one of these three things."

"Yes. OK."

He recites an official prayer as I weep with softening relief. I'm deeply freed by the simplicity. One thing to be grateful for and to photograph, each day. Go home and watch TV.

"Thank you, Father. I'm so thankful for this church."

I stand up. Just as I am opening the door, Father Mike jokes, "Don't wait another thirty-two years."

I laugh again and quickly do the math in my head. I don't have another thirty-two years, I'm pretty sure. But more importantly, he's not rebuking me for how long it just was. He's just inviting me to return.

And instead of metaphors for *return*, I will consider all the synonyms: To go back. Revisit. Come again.

Homecoming.

That night I pull back my comforter and get my laptop set up on my bed. I am freshly bathed, hair pulled back. Face serum on. I still can't believe I have permission to watch TV as a way to develop spiritually. I settle into the first episode of *The Chosen*. I want immediate emotion. Because I love intensity, get high on it, actually, I want instant epiphany. It doesn't come. The episode flickers with characters in shadowy passageways made of woven partitions, and so much pouring from earthenware jugs. It's all very historically deliberate and sensual. But Jesus isn't there too much, and I start to worry that I got my hopes up and shouldn't have. I've been numb, probably depressed, very alone these months of the pandemic. I begin to question why the priest recommended this.

It feels too long, the hour. And then Mary Magdalene, a disheveled beauty with curved cheekbones under matted hair, runs when Jesus comes through the door. Even as she tries to flee, hiding her face, gaunt with exhaustion, the hunch of her shoulders speaks of her self-loathing and shame. He calls to her. "Mary. Mary of Magdalene." She stops. She's been living her life as a lie, as Lily. Her expression is awash with fear. As she turns toward him, he opens his arms wide. "I will call you by your name." She collapses weeping into his embrace entirely, and he holds her without limit of time.

I'm crying too. I wonder what it would feel like to be held like that. I can't even bear to count up the years of only hugs; no one to hold me anymore. I have to take off my glasses and press my pajama sleeve to my eyes. I can't believe it could be so easy. To lie in bed in yoga pants and feel God.

Each episode has at least one scene that makes me cry, but a cry that cleanses, returning me to wholeness. And by wholeness, I mean a return to being opened enough to receive fresh hope. I fall in love with the opening credits, a choir of women singing to rhythms of an African-American spiritual: *Oh child, come on in, jump in the water…got no trouble with the mess you been.*

A two-dimensional gray fish swims from the left; then a teal fish from the right enters and swims horizontally. The gray fish pivots to follow; and it too, turns teal. More gray fish swim with them, unchanged, but others shift, and by the end of the song, a whole wheel of teal fish spins, an entire O. The lyrics then shift to the miracle: *Walk on the water.*

But I can't just let faith be. My judgment worms its way in. *The priest who suggested this to you must be a lightweight.* Come on—a television show? I don't know where that thought comes from, but there it is. Sure, he's a "nice guy," but maybe he gave me a fairly effortless penance because he doesn't really know how to dive deep. I know this sounds ridiculous that I would look upon him with such skepticism. These are the suspicions that come from the same place. The same pool. Doubt and cynicism lead me to judge. So while I recline under my comforter and watch a few more episodes and love them, I wonder about the "spiritual chops" of the priest who led me here.

• • •

I am in my "crash-landed pew" (where I collapsed when I first found this church, when "I myself was gutted like a fish").

It's Father Mike saying Mass. I know his name now. I'm curious to hear what he has to say, Mr. Lightweight.

Every priest has a different style. Some adhere closely to written homilies at the lectern, others freestyle it. In writing, this would be equal to "plotters"—writers who use detailed plot outline and sketches—and "pantsers"—writers who fly by the seat of their pants and just be in the moment and let the plots and story unfold free-style. Father Mike is a "pantser." He reads the Scripture and then puts on his headset to step down to the center aisle to begin his homily without notes. He doesn't shave his head like many other friars, and he sports a gray mustache that matches his eyes.

"Some of you might not know that ever since I came to St. Patrick's last year, I am here only half-time. The other half of the time I also go down to the border of Arizona to help migrants in the refugee camps. I just got back, and…"

How many times in my life will the joke continue to be on me? Here I am, thinking this guy recommended gratitude messages on the fridge and watching a heartfelt, artsy show about the Gospels because he's swimming in shallow waters. The opposite is true. I know next to nothing about refugee camps, and yet even within my ignorance, I grasp he's ministering to the crowds of broken and terrified. I'm deeply humbled by seeing how I minimize others, judge them, and put them into categories that diminish their worth.

Funny, but that wasn't in my confession. In fact, it wasn't even anywhere near my periphery. I'm blindsided—and deservedly so—by this sudden awareness. Now, I'm riveted by what Father Mike has to say.

> So my flight was canceled, and I had to wait a whole day to come home. I was exhausted and ended up in the only establishment near the airport, a dive. In the bar, the bartender started a conversation with me since I was the only one there.
>
> "So what brings you here?" the bartender asked.
>
> "I'm working at the border, helping out."
>
> "Really? I don't see why you would ever want to do that. Those people don't deserve to be here. Why are you doing that?"
>
> "My boss has asked me to."

At this, the congregation erupts into laughter through our masks. Father Mike's boss—God.

"Well," Father Mike continues, recounting the bartender's suggestion, "I think you should have a talk with your boss."

I'm not sure what sinks in the deepest. My mortification at how I minimized Father Mike and more than that, my investment in judging at all. But now I hear a story where this man committed to opening his heart to the marginalized shares his conversation from a dive bar where he let it be. He didn't try to prove anything, to win, didn't need to inform, change, or enlighten that bartender. And he certainly wasn't judging the bartender for his opposing views. So gentle. At that moment, Father Mike was a blossom of St. Thérèse's Little Way.

These blossoms have a way of strewing. In the weeks that follow, I am further stunned by my judgments when I read Father Mike's bio in the church bulletin. He spent five years as the chaplain of

El Abra Prison in Bolivia, has rebuilt homes affected by hurricanes in North Carolina, has walked as a Franciscan all over the world including Mexico, Morocco, the Philippines, and for many years guided a congregation whose parishioners came from one hundred different countries. And, in a final fact that underscores my ludicrous minimizing, he worked with youths in the slums of Peru.

• • •

With my judgments and resistance to my television penance fully gone, it begins to transform me. I'm up to the episode of *The Chosen* "The Rock on Which It Is Built." Again, almost an hour in, I am wondering, *When will I feel something?* Simon—let me be honest: the actor who plays him flashes a handsome smile. Not many people can pull off a short tunic, but with those legs and buff arms, he can. Quite well, in fact.

Simon, flooded with fear and desperation, has made shady business decisions to try to avoid utter financial ruin. As a fisherman, he's in soul-crushing distress. He's prayed and begged God, and still his nets have remained empty. He has one final night to change the course of his life. From midnight to dawn, the water laps on the side of his boat as he hopes, but nothing comes to him in the starlight except more bitterness rising within. When Jesus arrives at sunrise, and tells him to lower the nets, Simon balks, but doesn't want to disrespect his teacher. Jesus is steadfast: lower the nets. I'm impatient now. Rooting hard for Simon. Come on! Where are the fish? Are they ever going to come? I think maybe I read the wrong description of this episode.

Suddenly Simon is jerked so hard he falls forward, unable to control the taut edge of the net. Nearby, fishermen splash through waves, dashing to grab corners. "Pull up, pull up, pull up!" they all shout. Five men battle with their full strength to raise the bounty of fish flapping. As the entire boat overflows with fish scales blinking in the sun, the men have to jump out to keep it from tipping over. They're whooping and jubilant. On the shore, Mary Magdalene covers her mouth in awe. Jesus smiles briefly toward the sky with an expression of wonder.

There's no more hungering for hope, for now. Like all hunger, it will return. The abundance of the fish is not what breaks me open. What gets me is Simon falling to his knees on the shore. "You don't know who I am and the things I've done," he sobs.

Jesus kneels down to peer more closely at Simon, "Follow me."

As if brought by the sea wind blowing upon them, the woman from the opening credits—just a voice, no words, only the crying out of vowels—begins to sing.

I had planned on writing of a single miracle. That turned into two Multiplication of Loaves miracles, similar, almost identical. Those miracles didn't warn me that there'd be even more miracles coming, one spilling into the next like a water wheel with unstoppable momentum. Something is happening to me. I don't understand it. I feel more love rushing in my heart toward everyone with whom I interact. The people closest to me, and strangers.

• • •

It's twelve degrees out and I don't have enough get-up-and-go to drive into the city for Mass. Too much ice on my sidewalk, surrounding my car. Everywhere. I just don't have it in me to tiptoe over it all. I'm recovering from the time difference of just returning, thanks to the generosity of dear friends, from a trip to California. Truly an opportunity of abundance, it was the first time I'd ever been in my entire life. The lushness of Santa Barbara was staggering, the farmers' market alone, with buckets of sunflowers during winter. I'm sad I need to stay home this morning because I know today's reading is the Miracle of the Fisherman.

Where this thought arises from, I don't know, but I wonder what the Pope's insights are. Jetlagged and alone, surrounded by white sky, I'm able to head four thousand miles east, via the internet, and join the crowd in Rome. Ever since Mass went on livestream, and watching *The Chosen*, I'm getting used to the idea of holiness coming from my MacBook. I find the start of the Angelus as a camera turns to a single window in a block-long building, the curtains part to the swelling cheers, and Pope Francis wearing his little round hat pops out onto the balcony.

I'm entertained by all the people with arms open and flags waving, welcoming him to his own house. Talking about him is off-limits for me, and the reason is that people in my life (atheist, Catholic, Buddhist, and so on) have no problem letting me know what they perceive as his shortcomings and shortsightedness. I have no interest in defending anyone, including him. I respect Pope Francis as a writer. He has the gift of imbuing the simplest ideas with a soulful faith.

The crowd quiets. I listen to him in Italian as a woman translates into English. Also in the video alongside him someone translates into Sign Language. I love Sign Language. It's similar to when the choir sings in Latin, and the song sheet has Latin lyrics on the left (*laus et jubilatio*) and the English on the right (be praise and joy). I rarely understand it, but I find it fun to try and decode.

His voice echoes over St. Peter's Square.

> Every day the boat of our life leaves the shores of our home to go out into the sea of daily activities; every day we try to "fish in deep water," to cultivate dreams, to carry out projects, to live love in our relationships.... But often, like Simon Peter, we experience the "night of empty

nets"—the night of empty nets—the disappointment of working so hard and not seeing the desired results. Let us remember this: a poor, "ramshackle" boat is enough for him, as long as we welcome him… But do we—I ask myself—let Jesus get in the boat of our life? Do we make available to him the little we have?

Following the flow of the interpreter's motions, I find one word I think I understand. I Google it later to see, did I get it right? Yes, I know how to sign this. Boat: Two hands put together, cupped, as if empty, then bobbing a bit. It's the exact same gesture we make when receiving communion. Two hands. Put together. Letting him in the boat.

• • •

That day I knew he would be hearing my confession, I was so intimidated I thought Father Mike was seven feet tall. I return to church for the first time since my vacation to Santa Barbara. Father Mike is still a big guy, but not seven feet. He and Pat are generously welcoming people headed into Mass by opening the front doors wide.

"Hi!"

I am always happy to see Pat, a woman with soulful, sea-green eyes. When she looks at you, she both sees you and is at the same time 100 percent listening. "How have you been?" she asks.

"I had the chance to go to Santa Barbara! I visited the Franciscan Mission out there. It was so incredible."

Father Mike unhooks his mask and joins in our conversation. "That's where all the friars go!"

I nod. I knew all the friars pass through there, on their way to becoming Franciscans. I had fallen in love with that 250-year-old church. The exterior coral-pink columns and cream bricks, the interior awash in pale mango and mint, the Goya-style Spanish paintings on the walls, dramatic, full of mystery.

"The view is so incredible," I tell Pat. "It's like no other church I've ever been to. You get to the top of the front steps, turn, and bam!" I sweep my arm to conjure the Pacific, how it stretches in every direction. "The whole ocean is out there."

Father Mike opens his arms to indicate the expanse and agrees. "It's just gorgeous!"

"And every morning I walked up there, there were lemons and jasmine."

"Well," Father Mike pulls open the door of the church and jokes, "we don't have that here, but come on in."

The bells begin to ring so loudly that he won't be able to hear even if I shout. So I hurry inside, and as the bells keep on peeling I think, *But you do have lemons and jasmine here. You do.*

Moone

I turned to art, as I always do, in trying to understand the holy. The first thing that came to me initially as I dove into the miracle was a perfect carving of two identical fishes facing one another, just barely kissing. The only darkness in the granite is the indented curve of their mouths. Beneath them are five loaves as circles, and two angels, thin as stalks of wheat, standing on either side. With a bit more research, it became clear these focused images were part of a larger masterpiece, a sacred stone cross carved in tenth-century Ireland: The Moone High Cross.

Wow, that's beautiful, I thought. Then: Wait a minute. Don't I *know* this cross? Have I *been* there?

In 2007, I won a poetry prize of a trip to Ireland to study with writers. One afternoon, after our writing workshops, a priest took us out on a tour bus to see the holy sites. I recalled that this Celtic cross was notoriously challenging to find in the remote landscape of Moone, County Kildare. As a local, the priest didn't depend on the poorly placed signposts and hilarious directions ("If you come to a crossroads where the road seems to be tiny lanes, you are near it, but it's hidden"). We departed our bus and he guided us through mossy gaps in old stone walls; led us down overgrown, dappled footpaths. Eventually we came to the church, with three walls standing, one gone, the roof disappeared, now covered with Plexiglass. The centuries-old stone crosses of Ireland were vanishing, slowly washing away from acid rain.

In the center of the ruined abbey the eighteen-foot-tall Moone High Cross stood with a penetrating beauty. The priest shared, "The theme of this cross is God's goodness, how he comes to our need." I distinctly recall how he said those words with pride, then stepped away, just letting the images speak for themselves. Daniel in the Lion's Den. The Flight into Egypt. The Christ in the center of the Celtic circle had hands wide as wings. A raven carried bread to St. Anthony. All four sides were carved with deer, spirals, and birds.

Yes, I *had* been there and beheld this. And forgotten.

Is everything we need here? Do we just need to remember that? Is it like the boat in the vestibule at Light on the Hill? This is a nondenominational retreat center in the rolling hills of the Finger Lakes, where I had been going for over twenty years, including the three-year program in psychology and spirituality called *Finding Your Hidden Treasure*. By the front doors, in a lavender garden beneath a birch tree, a granite marker is carved with the Sufi saying, "I am a hidden treasure longing to be found." The indwelling.

As you enter the Inner Light Lodge, a gleaming wooden boat welcomes you alongside the benches where you sit to remove your shoes. A message on the tapered bow says monks in Thailand once used the boat. A hole cut into the bow held the "begging bowl," because monks depended on, and trusted, the kindness of others to help nourish them. In the Buddhist tradition, the "other shore" represents the journey toward enlightenment, but enlightenment was when you realized you were already *on* that shore.

This harmonizes with the image of Jesus found in many other representations. One of the most exquisite is a seventeenth-century relief, the Altar of the Back Choir, in the Cathedral of Seville, Spain (where I am certain I have never been). He emerges from white marble, extending his hand with a loaf, and at the same time, the other hand is already on the next loaf, ready to give. His arms are one long flow of giving, like a seashore; it just keeps on coming toward you, wave after wave.

Yes, I turn to art to try and understand the holy. Somehow, fragments hold on, like the Fat Fish I love, under centuries of ashes. Like the horror of one of the world's most beloved buildings burning in 2019. When Notre Dame Cathedral caught on fire, the Paris skyline frothed with smoke. The spire came crashing down, most of the roof was destroyed, and the church was essentially deformed. But the stained glass windows, with luminous imagery, survived. It's a miracle that these ruby stories of the miracles were untouched. Their glass winds of cobalt still blow. I can feel them.

All That Is Seen and Unseen

I planted morning glory seeds, not sure if the spot was sunny enough by the front doorstep with all the shade from the pines in this valley. As I poked the seeds into the loam with my index finger, I envisioned a cascade of heart-shaped leaves and a white trellis chock full of blossom. But the chipmunks stole my seeds and all I got were two weak, skinny tendrils that barely made it; I had to help them wrap around the black iron post, and I never got a trellis. Late August, just when I had given up on ever having blossoms, one cornflower-blue flower appeared. Then yesterday a deep purple morning glory burst from the vine. I was delighted. Today, two more appeared, undulating like wheels, twins. I wanted to take a photo because of the way the purple looked near my hanging lavender teardrop prism.

As I bent down to photograph the two blossoms and from the crouched angle, I caught sight of a third blossom hidden under a leaf. If I hadn't stopped, slowed down, and cherished what was there, I wouldn't have seen its hidden beauty. A trinity of blossoms in their perfect trumpet-silhouettes. How many times has there been extra, has there been abundance and I didn't see it, didn't know of it? How often did I tally the wrong score? How many times had I driven, singing along loudly with the Foo Fighters anthem that claims, guess what: you might not be seeing it all.

This is why we need one another so badly. We need to point things out to one another. That morning, I simply lucked out finding there was more. But for a moment, I was half-blind, like the grave keeper I met last Christmas Eve. I had that lighthearted flutter that day seems to bring, even with the heaviness of the pandemic. My task that morning was easy: head to the corner floral section of the grocery store and purchase two bouquets of a dozen roses for a pair of friends I was celebrating with later.

As I passed the outdoor shopping carts, an older man exited. Together we triggered the doors, and as they slid wide open in the frosty morning sun, I adjusted my mask and stepped back six feet to allow him to walk by. He carried a bag of chocolate truffles in one hand, and a festive bouquet of carnations in the other.

I greeted him. "Good morning! I'm here to buy flowers too!"

My words startled him, and his eyes, above his mask, shifted in expression. He hesitated. "Oh, yeah, well—these are for my wife's grave."

"I'm so sorry."

"Yeah, well, these are for her." He lifted up the nosegay. Plaid ribbons blew. "And these"—he shook the chocolates—"are for a lady friend of mine. We have been friends since childhood. She has Stage 4 cancer. She's got about four months to live. So…" he trailed off. His skin had an ashen undertone, like someone struggling with emphysema.

"Wow. That's a lot" was all I could muster. There were no words I could offer to lessen his pain.

He seemed relieved to talk, though. "I take care of all the graves at the West Simsbury Cemetery. I found a deep green bowl. I fill it with water and put it near my wife's headstone."

I tried to offer him a tiny hope about his bouquet. "Carnations last." We fell silent for a moment, in honor of her. "It's rough." I placed my hand over my heart, pressing on the down of my puffer jacket. "I have a deep faith, and that helps me, but you know, it can be hard."

The widower shook his head side to side. "It's too much. My wife's been gone for six years. My friend is dying soon. Faith? It's hard for me to find it. Sometimes I feel I've been given more than my share. I wonder, why me?" He shrugged. "Life."

I too, have asked, *why me?* I felt a kinship with him. "My dad died three weeks ago." I felt I was informing the pure blue sky and shifting clouds, in case they hadn't heard: my dad was gone. It still felt strange to form those words.

It was the man's turn to nod in understanding. More people entered the store, the wheels of their carts clanging; we had to end our interaction. "Well, I don't know if I will ever see you again," he said wistfully. "But it was nice talking to you. Good luck getting your flowers. They don't have much of a selection."

"Nice talking to you too," I backed away, waving with my mitten. "Merry Christmas."

Anxious, now, that the tips of all the petals would be browned, and the heads bent, I rushed through the aisles to get to the florist. But when I approached, it became immediately apparent to me that the Grave Keeper's grief had kept him from seeing. I could barely walk through the various tin buckets wet with white lilies in tissue paper. As if it were still August, batches of sunflowers stood with wide stems pressed tightly together in rubber bands. The floor overflowed with elegant mauve and blue poinsettias, dyed leaves twinkling with lilac and silver glitter. Glass refrigerator doors steamed with shelves of roses, the buds tightly whorled in colors that made me dizzy. Shell-pink, stained glass red, pale peach, and combinations of all three. The abundance surrounding me was the opposite of what the grieving man perceived. He was long gone from the parking lot, but I wanted to run after him and shout, "Come back!"

I didn't want to contradict him, to tell him he was *mistaken*. Because he wasn't. I just wanted to be alongside him both in the truth of his grief and in the truth of the nearness of beauty. Don't we all peer out at the world, sometimes, in the dim light of the widowed grave keeper?

It took me off guard, that abundance of Advent flowers in the floral section. It filled me with the exhilaration that comes after the ashes and emptiness of Lent, when I can finally walk into the church on Easter and know it is crowded with lilies because I can inhale their perfume before even seeing them. Their fullness always comes as a shock. No matter how much despair, or mornings of darkness, or destruction across the earth. No matter. God transcends it. We become like overflowing pots of Easter lilies, our faces like the blossoms looking every which way. A joyous crowd, looking around. Finding the divine everywhere.

But that's on Easter, when spring has come. What about all the days in Ordinary Time? The months between holidays and invitations? Or when we are shut down and crushed, and it's hard to perceive. The five thousand that were fed ate their fish, ate their bread. I don't know if they ever recognized how much was left over. I don't know if they vanished before they could turn around toward all that was overflowing and see.

Doublets

Two human figures (they are not angels since they have no wings).[3]

Gather the Fragments

I first became aware of doublets because of my curiosity about words spoken during the Eucharist: *Jesus Christ, who said to your Apostles, My peace I leave you, my peace I give you....*

This simple sentence baffled me. As a writer, I spend most days trying to not repeat my words in a single sentence. What is the difference between leaving and giving? Aren't they the same? Why does Jesus repeat it? Because, I learned, it's a doublet. Something doubled, so the meaning is reinforced, so it doesn't arrive with just one wing. It needs two to fly. The reassurance is all-encompassing. I paraphrase: *I will leave you this peace, and just in case you don't hear me, that I will leave it, I will also give it.*

Wings.

When I first began my learning about the Feeding of the Multitudes, I was confused, trying to keep the stories straight. The power of it is underlined by the fact that it's the only one of the thirty-seven miracles of Jesus to appear in all four Gospels — Matthew, Mark, Luke, and John. And then, in two Gospels, Jesus performs this miracle *twice*. First in Matthew 14, he feeds the five thousand, then right after that, in Matthew 15, he does it again feeding four thousand. In Mark 6, we hear of the miracle, and then again in Mark 8. I learned the name for these is *narrative doublet*. In all four of these miracles, Jesus says, "Gather the fragments." So many baskets overflowing. The baskets overflow (that is my doublet). At first, keeping the stories straight is a dance. It takes concentration to not be clumsy, grasping the pattern, but once you get it, it's like by putting your feet onto the diagram of shoes, you're dancing the two-step.

Two Fedoras

I only saw her once, and it was enough. Sitting a few rows behind me in church, with the most magnificent hat rising a full foot, probably more, atop her head. A distinguished cream-colored fedora with leopard-print ribbon around it. She wore the proudest expression, not haughty or vain, just pleased. Her makeup was also dramatic, fake lashes and jade eyeliner and rose lipstick. This sounds garish but it wasn't; she had a face you might find in a Manet.

When I turned to join the communion line, I welcomed the chance to casually stare as I headed her way. And to my astonishment and delight, she was actually wearing *two* hats, one stacked on top of the other. It was a bold move, yet it worked. She was the queen that morning. We got her message. It's a wonderful thing to wear one fashionable hat on your head! Why not double your joy and wear two?

Tide Tables

I've written of a perfect moment flooding me, within a sweet sun shower upon the medieval wall when I wept at La Cella, a hermitage where St. Francis once lived. Nothing's been the same since that late April afternoon in Italy eight years ago when I found out that peace exists inside me. I never knew it. But just because I know peace is possible within, and just because I crave its relief, doesn't mean I feel it as frequently as I wish I could. I have to take actions—my spiritual practices—and this invites the return. Where is there a chart, where I can anticipate when it might recede or rise? If only it could rush twice a day, like the incoming tide.

Peace Signs

All over the world the words at Mass are the same, just spoken in different languages. Before we eat the bread, the priest turns toward the people, extends his hands, and then joins them, saying, "The peace of the Lord be with you always." The congregation replies: "And with your spirit." The priest says, "Let us offer each other the sign of peace."

Then the peace doubles and doubles. We used to shake hands, but now after the pandemic we make eye contact, nod, and wave. I turn to the person behind me and say, "Peace be with you." I turn to the lady at the end of my pew, "Peace be with you." We give peace and we receive it, wishing it upon both the people we know and the strangers all around us.

The boys with their cowlicks sticking up—always two spikes of bed head, because they rushed to Mass late before their dads could wet the hair down—those little boys wildly shake their fingers in a V. They spin to offer it, giving to anyone who sees them in their circle, their peace sign of 360 degrees.

They remind me that peace is in church between people, and in nature. When I walk in the woods, I feel that I am the center of a wheel, and everything around me is exactly as it should be, in every direction, 360 degrees of nothing that needs to change. Nature has no questions or regrets. No resistance. No laments. Trees, land, vines, sky, clouds. Thoughts snag on branches, rip as I pray for those about whom I am worried. I walk for miles, letting go of my obsessions, gathering up peace. I think it's possible that hearing the wishes for peace from others leads me there, for as Hafiz says, "What we speak becomes the house we live in." Which is why the St. Francis Prayer begins, "Make me an instrument of your peace." So, for those minutes in church, we turn to one another, the rhythmic calling, perhaps how he reached out in his miraculous Sermon to the Birds—calling to them in Italian—*la pace, la pace.*

Mother Doublets

In a local coffee shop named Beanz and Co., I come for the eggs, enormous scones, caramel iced coffee, and also to support their mission of creating a workplace and gathering place for people with and without intellectual and developmental disabilities. It's like a club; all the members wear T-shirts that read the two words of their motto: "Everyone belongs." I first found this place after meeting a woman at a wedding who had tears in her eyes relaying to me that her son with autism works here, and it literally saved his life to have purpose. Most mornings a young woman greets me, much smaller than me (I am only 5'1" so I always notice those littler) who has Down syndrome. When you give them your order, you get a table marker with various words: *Gratitude, Peace.* You place *Hope* on your table and wait for your avocado on an egg to come.

Today two women intrigue me as I watch them talk. They're strangers to me; I still don't know many women in this town. But they have a bond, facing each other, louder at first, then lowering their voices, obviously discussing something private. One works here as a supervisor to the differently abled; the other has run in for a latte. Their hair color matches, both the shade of wet sand. The woman on the right has shaggy hair with her glasses tucked up on her head, and moves her hands through the air, making "up here" and "down here" gestures, high and low. The woman on the left, her hair short and stylishly buzzed, nods. Whatever they are speaking of, it's urgent, emotional, and intense.

I hear the woman on the right say, "She…she…she…baby."

I'm certain they're talking about one of their daughters. So one is the mother, but the other one clearly knows the daughter and loves her. As if the daughter belongs to both of them. I am positive that what binds them is that they've helped each other in the past as mothers.

Then they embrace so tightly they both squeeze their eyes shut and hold on. The embrace goes on for a long time. Pulling apart, they both open their eyes and wipe away tears. Every mother is a doublet, a story told twice.

Literary Doublets

There are passages from literature that impact you and stay within forever. At least for me, an eager early reader who grew into a writer, a bookworm whose grandmother praised my tiny cats-eye glasses because they made me look "brainy," certain childhood classics endure. A paperback of *A Tree Grows in Brooklyn* remains by my bedside, where, in my desire to live uncluttered and rather Zen in appearance, few other books reside.

The book opens in 1912 with the literal and metaphorical tree: "The Tree of Heaven…grew in boarded up lots and out of neglected rubbish heaps and it was the only tree that grew out of cement."[4] I love so many scenes and characters in this book, but I want to share one section. This passage of resiliency, in fact the entire novel, was born of Betty Smith's own immense childhood poverty. I have not ever suffered the sort of poverty illuminated here; I want to acknowledge that. After this year meditating upon the idea of abundance, I wanted to include this as an example of how attitude shifts everything. I'm not suggesting that positive thinking wishes away the unrelenting trauma of food scarcity or whisks away hunger pains. I offer this as an example of how perspective does impact how we see our lives, if sometimes only briefly.

In this most beloved masterpiece of twentieth century literature, the character of Katie Nolan — Mama — is pregnant and supporting her family as her tenement's cleaning woman. The other women in her neighborhood pity her for having an alcoholic husband, and thus having to get on her knees and scrub floors while full-bellied. Yet she is surviving with an original and mysterious approach to, of all things, coffee:

> There was a special Nolan idea about the coffee. It was their one great luxury. Mama made a big potful each morning and reheated it for dinner and supper and it got stronger as the day wore on. It was an awful lot of water and very little coffee but mama put a lump of chicory in it which made it taste strong and bitter. Each one was allowed three cups a day *with milk.* Other times you could help yourself to a cup of black coffee anytime you felt like it. Sometimes when you had nothing at all and it was raining and you were alone in the flat, it was wonderful to know that you could have *something* even though it was only a cup of black and bitter coffee.
>
> Katie defended her decision to her sister. "Francie is entitled to one cup each meal like the rest. If it makes her feel better to throw it away rather than to drink it, all right. I think it's good that people like us can waste something once in a while and get the feeling of how it would be to have lots of money and not have to worry about scrounging."[5]

Though it's been over a hundred years since the author's real mother dumped that cold liquid chicory out, every time I empty yesterday's coffee from the carafe and pour it down the sink, I think of this passage and offer a prayer of hope to the Katie Nolans kneeling all over the world.

• • •

You are the other half of the doublet here, Langston. This is for you. After a nor'easter, three degrees outside, there you are, through the branches, a gray crisscross of shadows, a lattice over deep snow. I'm thinking about your poem breaking through me and showing me what poetry could do, a small poster taped to the cinderblock wall of my ninth-grade science room.

> Hold fast to dreams
> For if dreams die
> Life is a broken-winged bird
> That cannot fly.
>
> Hold fast to dreams
> For if dreams go
> Life is a barren field
> Frozen with snow.

I loved your poem then, as I love it now. I was lost, scared, fourteen, drinking, and your message bolstered me every single day. Yes, the images are bleak, but you encouraged me to hold on to dreams: plural, not just one, but many, all of them. I didn't know that common motivational poster was the beginning of my long journey with you. These words are everywhere now; I'm certain you'd be pleased to know, still cheering us through days that sometimes are so hard we grope in the dark with dim nightlights.

But would it surprise you to learn that you, the famous poet Langston Hughes, a man who never had children, has helped me through decades of motherhood? We'd both agree you pulled from that well of memory, compassion, and imagination when you wrote "Mother and Son." Before I share it here with others, know there's so much I'd like to tell you, especially the uncanny way your words have reached me my whole life and been alongside me, including recently. I took down my old paperback of your autobiography (we call it a memoir now), *The Big Sea*, and turned before the Table of Contents and read, "Life is a big sea / full of many fish. I let down my nets / and pull." I had to laugh at the timing of this perfect epigraph.

I'm sure you remember the chapter called "Salvation," one of my favorite passages to teach. Every year, I copy it and pass it out to my students. It never grows stale, like all great art. The story of you being twelve, at your auntie's church, on a blistering night in the South where you were expected to join the other kids in being "saved," and you believed in what you had been told. Literally. That you would see Jesus! How you waited and waited while the congregation wailed and sang and prayed, and then you pretended you had "seen Jesus" and got up to be saved, just to get the crowd to stop. And how you cried that night because you had lied to your aunt, and no longer believed in Jesus because he never came.

My heart breaks every time I read it because I still want to see Jesus, too, and because you were just a child, with a child's mind, and you needed love. Jesus can be elusive, and that's an understatement. What is a Christian, really? Someone who tries to be there alongside others, to serve? I only know you spent your life writing about the souls of your people. Their beauty and dignity. How at the time of your early career, in the 1920s, a hundred years ago, the average Black person was only able to attend school up to the fourth grade. So you kept your writing simple, for those whose education hadn't had long enough to blossom. Anyone can fill pages with flourishing purple prose, but to pare life down to its essence? This is the mark of a genius. When you wrote in vernacular, you were ridiculed, yet you continued. Critics reviled you and called your poems the work of a "sewer dweller." Though you triumphed over it, these words provoke my anger still.

You kept writing from your truth, becoming the first Black writer to support themselves fully on their writing. You were the one who first fed us with the idea of dreams, the ones you carried out of that lonely childhood. I hope you know this; in my heart I hold the image of you as a child in a frigid rented room, cooking hotdogs on a hotplate, left alone while your mother toiled long hours as a waitress. How you discovered the beauty and healing magic of stories, of reading books, of how snow falling inside pages seemed as real as the snowfall outside.

You, as a mother, tell us the truth of what you have survived.

Mother to Son

Well, son, I'll tell you:
Life for me ain't been no crystal stair.
It's had tacks in it,
And splinters,
And boards torn up,
And places with no carpet on the floor—
Bare.
But all the time
I'se been a-climbin' on,
And reachin' landin's,
And turnin' corners,

And sometimes goin' in the dark
Where there ain't been no light.
So boy, don't you turn back.
Don't you set down on the steps
'Cause you finds it's kinder hard.
Don't you fall now—
For I'se still goin', honey,
I'se still climbin',
And life for me ain't been no crystal stair.

There have been times when I felt I had so little to offer my children, and now that they're fully grown, and I bemoan an outer lack of resources I long to give them, I think of you. How your poem uncovers the truth that abundance awaits, within. In the blend of vulnerability and wisdom born of my losses, frustrations, disappointments, and unmet desires. In my ever-beating love for them, I've taken that risk to let my guard down, speak face-to-face from the unvarnished place of who I really am, not as a heroine, but a human. Beyond layers of pride, inside, and underneath, lies the simple truth of the only mother I can really be.

The thing is, Langston, I still wish, many times, I could give my children a crystal stair. Just as the mother in you wanted that too. But it doesn't exist. What does exist is the ability to see the burden of life for what it is sometimes, and to follow in the word-steps of a mother to embolden and encourage my son, my daughter, myself. Don't you and I, together, know this is the way it always is? Returning to the mother for the strength to keep on climbing.

Outer Banks

Last summer I had the opportunity to visit a place I always longed to go. My whole life I'd wondered why people raved about the

Outer Banks of North Carolina. I flew in on a rainy night, and the following after-storm morning, as I approached the noon beach with Donnabeth, one of my oldest and dearest friends, I had to laugh that my question of *why* had just been answered in a heartbeat.

One afternoon Donnabeth drove us to the most spectacular spot facing the Sound, and she simply said, "Golden Hour." I don't know how this escaped me for so long, but I never knew this is a name for the light at sunrise and sunset. Before, I had always used *dusk* and *dawn*, but now I realized the lucidity of these two words. I took magnificent pictures as the sky shifted from gold to rose to the boldest, widest purple evening I'd ever beheld. We laughed together taking selfies, our faces awash in ochre light, the shore where a lifetime of friendship becomes both sea and sky.

Somehow even my phone knew the words, because a few months later, it put together a little movie for me, titled, "Golden Hour Over the Years" at the bottom of a picture of an Outer Banks sky. What could this be, I wondered, and clicked it. A montage of years of photos pulsated, all out of order. I wept at the beauty. I had no idea I'd taken so many photos of the sun going down. The only word for it is abundance, that I'd lived this many moments elated to be on this earth. Because that's what trying to capture the Golden Hour is. *Elation* to be on this earth. I don't think anyone can deny it.

I welcomed the way the images emerged and filled me with a sense of confusion. As someone who organizes obsessively as a way to cling to control, the absolute randomness left me breathless. Why strive to be so precise in my memory? What does it really matter, when I could follow the example of Mother Teresa (who took her religious name from St. Thérèse of Lisieux): "Put your past in the Sacred Heart and begin again in joy."

Just letting the images pop up as they did, no chronological or geographic order, was a lesson (one I apparently need over and over) to *let it be*. I'd recorded this hour of beauty everywhere. While stopped at a red traffic light, at an isolated rural post office under a tattered, pink-dappled sky. At my mother's camp on Lake Pennesseewassee, from her boat, first the disc of sun, then the burnished mountain ridge. Photos of fences under clouds appeared and I have no idea where that was. With my daughter and the dog Morty at the abandoned Medfield Psychiatric Hospital. Fields I am unsure of. Winter ice with holes in it, reflecting into smaller, nearer suns, at Nepaug Dam. Arroyo Burro Beach in Santa Barbara, the russet sunset lines under the evening star, really the planet Venus, like a later abstract of Georgia O'Keeffe, *The Beyond*. Haywire Farm throughout, sun illuminating watery hoof-shaped ripples of mud in the paddock and a white horse running toward me. Videos with the sounds of geese overhead in New England, a pink plastic bucket rolling in waves down South.

The stunning fact is that I had to look closer to distinguish between one of the most powerful spots I had ever been, overlooking the red edge of sun in Cortona, Italy, the day I realized for the very first time what peace was, followed by an almost identical photo of Fisher Meadow seven miles from my home. There was no coherence. Just an endlessly spilling Golden Hour filling up life with its glow.

> Life is the flight of the alone to the Alone.
> —Plotinus

What is there to express this morning but utter joy of this place, the Outer Banks? The sunrise over the ocean, its widening path of bright light coming right to me.

I walked last night down past the houses until there was only a wildlife refuge, dunes on the left, empty beach on the right. It was not really "empty." So what is "empty"—that hunger within?

We think there is nothing there. But what if we're full of sea grasses and long-legged birds trotting in the gifts of the sea, being fed, trusting in the bounty of the foam sizzling, hissing as the wave recedes?

What if the empty place within is a place we would actually sacrifice to travel to? A place where houses, lamplight, people recede as well?

What if you kept contentedly, even joyfully, walking into that space of what could be called desolate, solitary, uninhabited?

If you let this place inside show its ecosphere? Its air and light, its vastness?

If you let that spaciousness inside, which you have so long feared, reveal how many miles it actually is?

You were always so afraid of the emptiness taking you over, taking you down.

But now, no longer troubled by it, it can show you its beauty, so big you cannot see where it leads, nor where it ends. You can never give enough thanks for the emptiness; it surrounds you so fully. Now, no longer denying it, it turns itself inside out. You're hungry, running, free, alive. You're airborne.

The Gathering

Miracles

Why, who makes much of a miracle?
As to me I know of nothing else but miracles,
Whether I walk the streets of Manhattan,
Or dart my sight over the roofs of houses toward the sky,
Or wade with naked feet along the beach just in the edge of the
    water,
Or stand under trees in the woods,
Or talk by day with any one I love, or sleep in the bed at night with
    any one I love,
Or sit at table at dinner with the rest,
Or look at strangers opposite me riding in the car,
Or watch honey-bees busy around the hive of a summer forenoon,
Or animals feeding in the fields,
Or birds, or the wonderfulness of insects in the air,
Or the wonderfulness of the sundown, or of stars shining so quiet
    and bright,
Or the exquisite delicate thin curve of the new moon in spring;
These with the rest, one and all, are to me miracles,
The whole referring, yet each distinct and in its place.
To me every hour of the light and dark is a miracle,

Every cubic inch of space is a miracle,
Every square yard of the surface of the earth is spread with the
    same,
Every foot of the interior swarms with the same.
To me the sea is a continual miracle,
The fishes that swim—the rocks—the motion of the waves—the
    ships with men in them,
What stranger miracles are there?

—Walt Whitman

One Dewdrop

Outside my house is a bank of snow. It won't melt for another month or two. Under it awaits the ever-spreading blanket of lilies of the valley that will appear in May. Hardly anything brings me as much pleasure as that field of tiny, sweet bells. I am not a gardener, so I'm extra-pleased by the way they take care of themselves, untended, having found the perfect spot to flourish. It only happens a few nights of the year, but when the conditions are right, after a warmer spring afternoon hovering a bit above seventy degrees, the breezes of dusk rise with their warmth and swirl, all the way around my shed and up to the second floor, their scent wafting through my window and filling the dormers of my room.

I say this because today I alighted on a truly exquisite paragraph from St. Thérèse of Lisieux from her autobiography, *Story of a Soul*. St. Thérèse is new to my life, an absolute gift, spreading and filling in the bare spaces of my losses. Though a beginner in reading her work, I suspect my twenty-five years of teaching writing to teens has prepared me for the passionate, encompassing texture of her prose. She was a mystic, yes, but she died at twenty-three, so young. Her writing bursts with the falling, then soaring, emotional flights of adolescence.

Falling in love with St. Thérèse is like joining a new club. I had wondered who she was, this statue in the entrance of nearly every Catholic church, or near the votives, always cradling a crucifix and a bouquet, and cupping one rose in her hand, offering it. I knew she was named "The Little Flower," but why was she there? Sometimes people think Catholics know the entire cast of characters, but we don't. I passed by her for years, a stranger I recognized, but we were never introduced.

I rely on certain passages from the psalms as my daily guide; most essentially, the words from Psalm 119:105: "Your word is a lamp for my feet, a light for my path." At the end of 2021, as I was leaving to drive the two hours home on the Mass Pike from my daughter's place outside Boston, the thought came to me, "I wonder how far I am from that shrine I read about. I wonder if it's even worth stopping by." The thought came from "nowhere." Just idling in my car eating an Everything Bagel in the parking lot of the drive-thru of the Dunkin Donuts. I had learned a lifetime ago that in the parking lots of fast-food chains, my life can change direction. The "sacred" isn't something separate from the everyday. So I shouldn't even put sacred in quotation marks. But I constantly have to remember that it isn't separate from a medium coffee with two sugars and two creams; it's got wings attached.

Consulting Google maps, I committed to the easy, rural drive past sadly broken-open barns on back roads. When, forty-five minutes later, just as my GPS announced, "You have arrived at your destination," at the same moment I spied her. St. Thérèse stood sculpted of gorgeous, old-world Italian marble. It was impossible not to feel she had been waiting there for a long time to welcome me with that rose. In retrospect I see how that one simple statue of St. Thérèse literally opened up to an embankment of petaled possibilities. As if at a collective party, everyone was invited to attend, milling around. Our Lady of Guadalupe painted in gleaming Mexican colors near the field. Our Lady of Fatima with the three children kneeling before her. A Garden of Saints, carved white shapes, curved in a semicircle. Throughout, there are funeral prayer cards others have left behind, faces of deceased uncles, sisters, mothers, cousins, sons and daughters, wrapped in rosaries, bound to the votive candles so their memory wouldn't blow away.

What plants the shrine with peace is that local people have tended it for a hundred years. No one famous, no one fancy, just generations of Little Flowers in the smallest of the fifty states at the first shrine in the entire world devoted to St. Thérèse.

Like all living things, The Shrine of the Little Flower loses leaves, grows new buds. There are conversations about moving St. Thérèse down the hill, to surround her with roses, though they are difficult to grow in New England. The older paths are being updated so visitors in wheelchairs can glide smoothly around and through. Along the red shed in the back, rakes lean for anyone to use, should they want to assist after they've stopped by for some midday solace with their sandwich.

Something caught my attention that first visit. Clipped to the spears of the low iron fences bordering the statues, clear plastic folders held typed stories, printed out in a large font. They bobbed in the wind like sheets pinned to a laundry line. I only vaguely registered that these were the recorded miracles that have occurred there. Silvia, the shrine's director, had explained what the papers were during her tour, but their contents were a mystery to me. In the weeks following that day trip, a curiosity sprouted: what *was* being held in those sleeves?

I emailed Silvia and she directed me to Sister Grace, who collected all the archives of the miracles. When Sister Grace agreed to meet with me, I eagerly returned within the next week to the unpretentious church at the shrine, converted from a plain brick elementary school that looked just like the one I attended as a child. Outside a modest house in the back, where Sister Grace resides, the sign for the gift shop hangs. The shop, no larger than a three-season porch (which I think it once was) features the writings of the saint and biographies about her. Last time there, I purchased a rosary of periwinkle crystal beads, very round. You get to know any rosary not by sight but by touch.

Tending the bookstore had been Sister Grace's ministry for many years. I found myself in a room behind the store, sitting with her at a table, as she prepared to read from a stack of miracles, the ones I had at first overlooked, strung around the shrine.

I asked, "How did you become the steward of these stories?"

"When I met visitors outside or when they came into the gift shop, I would often just, you know, casually, no pressure, say, 'Oh you must have a special devotion to St. Thérèse.' And oftentimes without me saying anything more, they would tell me how she had helped them and interceded in a powerful way in their lives. So I made this collection, and one of the parishioners typed them up."

Sister Grace wears a white, cotton veil on her head, a cream-colored sweater with pockets that has stretched out to the length of a duster, a white dress with a midi-length hem, and white tights with the weft of tube socks. Her fair skin holds peace and light. No makeup, no photo filters, an older, unadorned face. How I wish more people could witness the truth that sometimes when a woman devotes her entire life to seeking radiance, a radiance descends. Like the sun diffused through a curtain, a glow you can look at directly. And I find this comical: the natural color of her lips are the same shade as the Brick-oh-la Mac lipstick I just bought at Ulta.

She continues, "And then some say, 'Oh yeah and St. Thérèse really has done a miracle in my life.' I would say 'Do you feel comfortable telling me?' I don't pressure them."

"You invite them."

"I invite them."

"You are put in the role of holding people's stories."

"I always wanted to have a tape recorder, but it never worked out. I wanted to record the stories, but instead I just had to listen. I had to really listen."

I felt a kinship. Through the decades I taught creative writing—the thousands of stories, spoken, sobbed, abandoned, revisited, written, held—trust had to be cultivated first. A sacred trust. A scarce trust. Sister Grace had checked her notes to make sure she had permission to share them. I respected how she offered her protection.

There's nothing I love more than being read aloud to. My mother was a loving mother but not demonstrative; of the few memories I have of being near her, one of them is when she read picture books to me. As I dreamily stared at the lace curtains on the windows, soothed by Sister Grace's voice, I recalled how, together on the couch, I'd press myself into my mother at the first line of Janice May Udry's *The Moon Jumpers*: "The sun is tired." On my fireplace mantel now, I prop up one of Maurice Sendak's illustrations from that classic, a brother and a sister pretending to fly, looking so free together. They symbolize my own children.

Most of the miracles Sister Grace shared were the length of prose poems; others spilled onto two pages. They were stirring, absolutely beautiful, many of them about people crying themselves to sleep over dire medical circumstances, cancers of the body, and problems of both newborn and aging hearts. Interspersed with CAT scans and MRIs, doorbells rang with deliveries of rose bouquets. A grandmother awaiting her ultrasound result was given the one yellow rose from the yard, plucked by her grandson. Birthday cakes arrived with purple sugared roses. Kitchens filled with the overwhelming aroma of roses as the phone rang with news that the transplant organ is found.

"It takes such bravery, don't you think? To experience these things, and to go forward with it, to put it out there. Do you agree?"

"Mmm-hmm. Yes," she said nodding.

"Because of the fear of being thought of as crazy, it takes that bravery to say, 'This is what happened to me.' A real place of strength."

"Yes," she said as she considered my words. "And it keeps getting better and better. This is the story of Suzanne, but I call her Eileen," Sister Grace began another one. "Both she and her husband have gone home to the Lord."

• • •

A beautiful woman named Eileen arrived at the shrine with her husband at 9:00 a.m. on a cold January morning. She was fearful and quite distraught. In tears she recounted how the doctor had told her in November that there were a phenomenal number—forty-six—malignant tumors on her liver, and there was nothing they could do for her. She had about two weeks to live. But here it was, January, and she was still alive. She still had the tumors, and that is why she had driven two hours to get to the shrine, to ask for God's help through the intercession of St. Thérèse. She was very frightened.

"I had a very busy life," she explained. "I went to church but only when it was convenient, and that wasn't very often. Now, I've returned to the sacraments; I promised God I would go to Mass every day. My husband has made the same promise. Some friends told me I should come to this shrine to venerate the relics of St. Thérèse and pray that the tumors would disappear."

Eileen had a relic of St. Thérèse. The following summer she and her husband returned to the shrine. Eileen was a new person. Joyful, confident, faith-filled, and always wearing her little relic of St. Thérèse. Her physical health had not returned to normal. Though some tumors had disappeared, a small number of tumors remained on her liver. But her *fears* had disappeared. And she had become a true apostle, spreading her love of God and St. Thérèse to everyone she met. The miracle given Eileen was far more wonderful than what she had asked for. And Eileen herself realized this. Her husband explained it to me in this way.

When I came home from work one day, and asked Eileen how her day had been, her answer surprised me. She told me in a gentle and steady voice, "I went to the funeral parlor today. I made all my arrangements. Even my clothing. You know how much I love jewelry. The only thing I want to be buried with is my relic of St. Thérèse."

Roger's voice shook in awe as he recounted this. "It was a new Eileen." She was no longer the fearful, distraught wife he had brought to the shrine nine months before.

St. Thérèse had said, "I will let fall from heaven a shower of roses. I will not look down from heaven, I will come down." And she had. Eileen was no longer afraid, because Thérèse was right there with her, instilling faith and confidence. A companion on the journey.

• • •

How familiar this woman's struggle was. I once had a large, cancerous tumor and knew what it was to be filled with fears. "I love this story. The idea of, well, maybe if you could shrink my tumors, that would be great, but your fear is shrinking, that's good. You will be taken care of. Sometimes our prayers are answered but not in the ways we expect."

I turned my attention to the display on construction paper, a Day in the Life of the Carmel, which showed the schedule of the French cloister of Thérèse. That she started her day with prayer at 4:00 a.m.; that she ate the worst of the leftovers without complaint.

I realized I'd come to ask Sister Grace one particular question and nervously spoke it. "Why would some people get a miracle, but not other people?"

Sister Grace impressed me deeply in how effortless this answer was for her. Her tranquil delivery continued. "Well, it has to be, you know, God's plan for us. God's plan for us is the best plan; we cannot plan something better for ourselves than what he has planned. You know, St. Thérèse trusted our Lord and said that if you prayed for her she would intercede like the Wedding at Cana. Our Lady said to her son, 'We have no more wine.' She didn't tell him what to do, how to solve the problem, OK? She just brought him the problem. I mean who in their wildest imagination would come up with water changing into wine?" She laughed.

I had not expected her to talk about the miracles of Jesus. The Wedding at Cana was, in fact, his first one, and I had never given it much thought. There were miracles I kept on the periphery, sometimes because they seem so far-fetched. That just shows the contradictions in my faith—often a bit ridiculous, I think. I don't know why I believe in some and not others. I drove all that way to listen to her, and knew, at that moment, that Sister Grace was widening the aperture through which I view the divine.

"God's plan for us is so much bigger and beyond our thoughts, and so Saint Thérèse said that she would be like Martha, at the death of her brother Lazarus. Lazarus was four days in the tomb, and you know, Martha said to Jesus, if you had only been there when my brother was sick, but Jesus went so far beyond. Having Lazarus come out of the tomb. That was a far greater miracle than if he had come out when he was sick. So we have to trust God's will, and his love for us, that is beyond our imagining."

She flicked the corners of all the pages. "Such an abundance of stories. A lot of the people who come here, it's phenomenal, really, a shower of roses. No matter how many you have, there's so many more." She swept her open hand over them like a gesture to indicate a panorama. "Roses, roses, roses."

The clock in the other room chimed two. "I have to take Bill home now, do you mind?"

"Of course not."

Bill, an older man with a serious expression, entered the room. Sister Grace took care of him some days. She slipped his arms into his windbreaker, then helped him zip it.

"She's a fast driver," he said somberly. "You don't want to drive with her."

"I didn't know that," I responded. "Thanks for the warning."

"Wise guy," Sister Grace said and smiled.

Bill made a sound of tires squealing.

She laughed. "It drives Bill crazy, because I like to stop. We have these beautiful swans." She began to pack up. "Here, I made you copies." She handed me my own stack of the printed, stapled miracles from which she had read.

I was honored and slipped them into my backpack. She and Bill and I headed out; I was reluctant to leave the grounds. This was my third visit in just a few months, and every time I wanted to stay. I love the view of the empty fields, so I settled on a bench at Our Lady of Fatima, joining the statues of the three children praying to her. I guess I was the fourth child. My phone buzzed, and since no one else was around, I wasn't disturbing anyone, I took the call. My daughter and I had a lighthearted conversation about one of our favorite reality shows on Netflix, the new season that just dropped. *Selling Sunset* was complete and utter trash, but talking about its trashiness made us laugh.

Yakking on my cellphone about mindless TV while also being part of the the miracle of Fatima, when Our Lady appeared to shepherd children in Portugal. As someone who seeks out the holy, it's so easy to think it's a place that must be found. It's a paradox. Yes, there are holy places—this shrine, Assisi, the indwelling of many churches—but in fact, everything is holy. There is no map that exists that shows the delineation between the ordinary and the sacred. Because it's all one. The Divine is everywhere. The spots we wrongly conclude are just temporal are temples. I know firsthand what it is to be found in the cathedral of McDonald's golden arches.

To find St. Thérèse is opening a door into a dwelling filled with all sorts of other doors that await. It's like one of those dreams where you are in your house, even though you've never been there before, and you discover, with glee, that your house has rooms that were heretofore hidden. Here, St. John of the Cross's discussion of the Divine captures Thérèse as well: "For He is like an abundant mine with many recesses, containing treasures, of which, for all [who] try to fathom them, the end and bottom is never reached;

rather in each recess, [seekers] continue to find new veins of new riches on all sides."[6]

St. Thérèse of Lisieux was a poet mystic whose lush writing I'm guessing might be off-putting for some readers, and I get that. But I welcome its intensity. I can only take in a few paragraphs of her autobiography at a time, it's so rich. I don't read it linearly but allow myself to alight. And so I have made a circle here, returning to where this chapter began: little flowers. This is her writing to her sister:

> My Little Celine,
>
> You must always be a drop of dew hidden in the heart of this beautiful Lily of the valley…The dew-drop—what could be more simple and pure?… It is born beneath the starry sky, and survives but a night. When the sun darts forth its ardent rays, the delicate pearls adorning each blade of grass quickly pass into the lightest vapor.… One must be so little to draw near Jesus, and few are the souls that aspire to be little and unknown.… He has become the Flower of the field to show how much he loves simplicity.… The Lily of the valley asks but a single dewdrop, for which one night shall rest in its cup.[7]

We live in a world where everyone wants to have their worth magnified by an audience, to be validated with thousands, even millions, of followers on social media. We're swept into the lies of constant comparisons, measurements, and numbers, knocked down by the falsehood that only the "biggest" of anything can matter. Money. Attention. Affluence. Excess. No wonder we suffer from low self-esteem, apathy, and despair. I, too, am vulnerable to becoming twisted up by these harsh values. But in the fragrance of St. Thérèse, I embrace the truth and beauty of who I am.

A drop of dew. I'm little.

However Many Marys You Need

A few years ago at work, while talking over the rhythmic noise of the Xerox copier shooting out paper in the faculty lounge, my dear friend Chris and I were eating lunch. I shared with him that I felt self-conscious of how many Marys I was wearing.

"Is something wrong with me? OK, so I've got the Mary tattoo, hidden now, but there's also this Miraculous Medal around my neck, and an Our Lady of Grace bracelet. I mean, how many Marys does it take?"

Chris didn't hesitate to answer. "However many Marys you need."

I had to laugh at his certainty. Whatever crazy thoughts I had before, his confident answer quelled them. I trust Chris implicitly. He was my student over fifteen years ago, when we bonded over our mutual admiration and respect for the haiku of Richard Wright, and then, after he graduated from art school, Chris became my colleague. Nothing is as meaningful as witnessing a student grow up and then grow into becoming a teacher alongside you. He is of Puerto Rican descent with grave brown eyes, a woolen cap playfully perched crookedly on his head. Anyone who knows Christopher Roque knows this: His expression is pensive one minute, lighting up in a welcoming smile the next. His earlobes, wide with expanders, give the impression he's easy to see through, but that's not true. Chris is very complicated and full of questions about life. He says nothing lightly.

I've known many, many creative people in my life, and Chris is one of those rare talents who excel at both visual art and writing. Usually it's one or the other. But Chris's whole life is about commitment to craft as a teacher, painter, poet, son, brother, lover, and friend. I wish I could reproduce his paintings here, because so much dissipates when translating paintings into words; I am in a constant state of feeling thwarted as a writer in describing images of all sorts.

I once stood spellbound in front of one of Chris's works at Gallery on the Green. He had taken an insignificant brush, like one used to polish shoes or groom a horse, and transformed it, placing it in a holy shaft of light, rendering the ordinary sacred. Then, last Saturday at a pop-up art show in an industrial section of the city, I encountered *Sleeping Beauty*, another one of Chris's works, this time a nude, head turned away. At first I thought a baby-blue scarf dangled along the figure's spine, but then I realized it was a line of blue light grazing her. The side of her breast curves into the bare, voluptuous ochre landscape of her back, the miracle of the sienna in her skin.

This commitment to capturing the beauty of life is also encoded in his work as a writer, in the truths of his own haiku:

A tidal wave goes
In and out, so close and far.
Just like how love moves.

Everything I learned
Does not compare to the things
That I had to feel.

Because of Chris's shoring me up, I happily let in all the Marys, now placed around my home like nightlights. The greats never cease to feed me. The Michelangelos. The Fra Angelicos. The Lippi *Mother and Child* with the Blessed Mother's delicate mantilla, sewn of silver or silk, how it falls so long it turns into a sash around the waist of her baby, so translucent you can hardly see it circling. I could not pick a favorite Mary, because they, too, keep on circling, appearing. It would be like choosing a favorite mountain view or skyline. The one you love best is the one you're beholding.

There's a Mary that's gotten me through the recent hard times, having found myself so exhausted and desperate for the simplest of images, when prayer becomes too hard. *Mary Untier of Knots* is a painting from 1700 Germany by Johann Georg Melchior Schmidtner. Essentially, Pope Francis came across her in the 1980s and shared her, and she's been embraced by Latin America ever since, now treasured worldwide. Surrounded by the childlike faces of angels, she stands calmly under the seeping yellow light from a dove, her head tilted to gaze down at a white ribbon she's untangling. The knot she's working on is free, opening wide, and vanishing; the ribbon is smooth once again. An angel on her left holds the end of it, stares out at the viewer, trusting this detangling with his whole heart. The expression on his face says: "She's got this."

The angel on the right is holding the ribbon still weighed down by knots. What are my problems, my heartaches? Each is a knot. The prayer to her is simple: *I entrust into your hands the ribbon of my life.* I keep this phrase on my to-do list on my phone, a permanent reminder of things I need to accomplish. And there is grace in the asking, not just the answering. I can't do it alone. When I untangle things, I escalate with frustration, pulling the knot even tighter, becoming angrier. Mary doesn't start pulling the knot with her teeth, like I do. Or poking at it with a needle. Or giving up. Still, letting go is hard. What of the situations that are bound so tightly I cannot see any movement? They just go on and on, and keep hurting. Is she working to untie them? Like a mom, does she lean down and say, "Here, honey, let me see. Let me try. Little bee, hand it over."

I decided to post her on my Instagram site. I don't think of what I do on social media as "religious," but others have told me they think it is. I guess posting pictures of Mary *is* religious, but to me, it's just my life. In the text underneath, I told the story of how Chris's words impacted me, and I also wrote:

> I would share here the list of knot-problems I have recently asked for help in undoing, but they are personal, and only Mary and my closest friends know. Instagram isn't the place to reveal what the tightest, hardest knots are. We all need a mother to turn to. Well, I guess I should speak for myself. I need one. Here she is, the ribbon unspooling in her hands.

I sometimes post things and get no responses, but this Mary received lovely comments. Interestingly, the comments were from those who consider themselves religious and others who do not, and I could not tell them apart:

"I need Marys too! I always will!"

"Such patience and mercy! I should have a few more Marys!"

"I love how everyone is basking in her, but she still looks so humble! I love this painting now too!"

And then a comment from Chris.

> An honor to share space, time, and our religious beliefs together. Your line, "We all need a mother to turn to," just pierced me. Ugh,

Maureen, how I appreciate mother Mary allowing me the opportunity
to explore the themes of sensitivity and vulnerability. How our mother
is the greatest example of those two things...

When the next Mary enters, it's in the basement gathering hall
of an old maritime monastery in Maine. It's homey, and by that
I mean I am more and more aware of the places where I feel *at
home*. Years ago, in my divorce, when I lost a house that had been
my cherished home, it became absolutely essential that I find other
places, besides my new house, to feel a sense of belonging. I feel it
here, with a sense of humility, honored to be invited among their
parish to talk about my book.

I mill around during our coffee hour, appreciating the array of
modest decorations, especially the photo of St. Thérèse of Lisieux
atop the microwave. In the corner, on a wall of wooden paneling,
hangs an enormous oil painting of the Holy Family. Mary is draped
in a lilac headscarf, her face an oval, eyes lowered so much they are
almost closed, indicated by two black lines. Her face is rendered
well enough, as are Joseph and two lambs, but it's the baby who
dazzles.

You don't see this often, not in hundreds of years of medieval icons,
not in centuries of Renaissance art: Jesus actually resembling a real
newborn. He's often standing upright, already a toddler, frequently
luscious and plump, a hefty infant in Mary's arms. But this Christ
Child has a face of the freshly born, still squished. The way his
body nestles against her is also realistic, the weak neck and the
heaviness of the head. The focal point of the work is his left hand
grabbing on to his mother's sleeve, long mauve lines indicating
just how tightly his fist is clutching. In a final bold, contemporary
touch, a brushstroke of white paint suggests the plastic mother-
infant hospital identification bracelet on his wrist. Someone in the

group tells me this is the work of an old woman, a member of the parish, who has recently passed.

An hour later, we are beneath Mary, around tables we've moved into a square to be together, sharing about how the psalms of lament describe the darkest hours of our lives. The woman sitting next to me is named Teresita. She's been watching me closely, but not in an intrusive way. More like something is burning inside, and she's waiting to see if she should show us what's singeing her.

Josie, the woman to my left, asks me, "You seem to get a lot out of Psalm 23. But I've never felt God like that. I've never felt he came to protect me." I'm stumped by her words. Faith is hard. Here she is, having spent years of her retirement volunteering at this monastery, feeling God has not come for her, when her neck glows with the gold of a chain and a crucifix. She is devoted to God, yet has not felt protected.

I start sharing about how my understanding of the word *shepherd* is what shifted me, when Teresita raises her hand quickly, the way we used to in those old-fashioned hearing tests, wearing headphones, *lift your hand if you hear a sound in one ear.* She is so near me I can see the aqua-blue veins in her wrist. Josie's words have impacted her.

We turn to Teresita.

"When my daughter died, I was so angry." She stops while we all take this in. The room is so still we can hear the sea.

"Well, I'm still angry." She pauses. We give her all the time she needs. "I will probably always be angry. I prayed and prayed after her death. But I got nothing. No relief. Finally, I couldn't take it anymore. I just said, 'Look, I want to talk to your Mother.'"

All of us around the table laugh, a warm, connected laughter. We all need a mother. And it's funny, too, because the phrase "I want to talk to your Mother" also sounds like disciplining a child in trouble, heading straight to the source to set the record straight.

"It was a closed casket," she adds.

She never saw her daughter again. There's a feeling in the room. It's love. I'm among gentle people who recognize, in Teresita, an infinitely gentle, infinitely suffering thing. We listen to one another breathing and hear the crashing of the sea. No one asks her when this tragedy happened. The timeline does not matter. Grief uncoils and never in a straight line.

She shares with me, later during the book signing, that her daughter died in Ireland, and now she feels called to go there, to that exact spot where her daughter passed. She has never been there. When I sign her book, I write, "I hope you get to Ireland!" and I draw lopsided hearts beside a scraggy cross.

Then we all enjoy steaming bowls of Italian Wedding Soup together. My eyes lower, observing the shape of Teresita's hands. One curls around her spoon as she scoops the broth and meatballs. Her other hand is grabbing her napkin in the exact same way the baby in the painting above her is gripping his mother.

Feeling so lonely
Even though I am with you—
Lonely, one can feel.

What's a mother's love?
It's gasping for air, fresh air,
While wishing for more.
—Christopher Roque

A few months after meeting the woman who wanted to speak with Jesus' mother, I have the opportunity to return to Italy. I am beside myself with gratitude. I joked with people how it didn't seem possible, that I wouldn't believe it until I heard the bells of Assisi. And then, suddenly, though the countdown of days took forever and my travel time was twenty-three hours, I am standing in a medieval stone street as the bells keep ringing. My trip is centered around writing and praying. The first thing I do the night after I arrive in my incredible apartment is head to Santa Maria delle Rose, for a permanent exhibit called *Maria* by Guido Dettoni della Grazia that I did not see when I was here six years ago.

As I enter the exhibit, I feel as if, in the years since Chris said, "However many," somehow I was headed right to this spot all along. There are thirty-three hand-carved Marys, in thirty-three types of wood, all the same size, able to fit in the palm of the hand, but each ensconced in its own glass tube filled with light. The tubes hang in a crescent row.

The artist discovered this flowing shape in wax in his hand while blindfolded. He felt it. That was the prototype. Now it's multiplied; every single Mary has this same shape, changing identity at five various angles:

with the Child in her arms
she carries the pitcher to the well
kneeling at the Annunciation,
she is expecting
the dove of Peace

As you walk around all the Marys, they keep changing, depending on which Mary you are viewing, and from what perspective.

Written on the wall in eight languages it reads: *The hands are a haven where I learn to invoke you.* In the center, the artist has provided four carved Marys for the viewer to hold. These are made of white marble. I pick one up. It's cool and medicinal. When I hold her in my right hand, she fits easiest into my palm when she is the dove. I hold her in my left hand where she fits best as *Incinta*. She is expecting. *Incinta*.

One Mary has wood grain like dark water widening around her back as if someone dropped a stone upon her spine.

One has the grain like rain racing down glass.

One is mysteriously obsidian, hidden.

One is distinctly littler than all the other thirty-two.

One looks stippled with needles.

One has lines like sheet music.

One has wood grain like light rays spraying all over her body.

One is striped like a brown zebra.

One has the center of grain in the mandorla shape of a woman giving birth.

How many Marys do we need?

One with gouges in her heart.

One a sandpapered blur.

Sac Red Heart

In the sunny Piazza del Comune, the center square of Assisi, I shift over on the stairs away from the ancient two-tiered fountain because when the spring wind gusts, I get blessed with its falling water droplets. I fall into a cheerful conversation with a group of already sunburned Irish people sitting under an umbrella at the cafe, declining their invitation to take a chair at their table several times, then I shyly join when they keep insisting.

"I'm Maeve, that's Nora, Finn, and Barry."

I say my own name and clap my hand over my heart for emphasis, having barely spoken to anyone in English for three days, and relying instead on exaggerated gestures and pantomime to communicate.

"Maureen?" Maeve asks. "Are you Irish then?"

"Partly. Maureen Mary Mary O'Brien, because my Protestant mom didn't know that a Catholic confirmation name wasn't supposed to be the same as the child's middle name."

They all laugh and tell me they are in Italy to celebrate Nora's fiftieth birthday, which happened two years ago, but they had to cancel the plans until now due to the pandemic. I nod. My feelings about my own fiftieth birthday are a silent predawn inside me: I awoke in Hartford Hospital to my surgeon telling me he got the pathology report that morning, and I would need more surgery but he believed he got all the cancer out. I was given a second chance, first with addiction, then with cancer, my life now a double doublet.

They're quite inquisitive about me, and enthusiastic about the book when I tell them why I am in Assisi all alone. They're clever conversationalists and leap around topics with wit and curiosity. One of my favorite things about traveling is that friendships are accelerated, forming very fast. They are from Northern Ireland, and Barry explains to me—a quick sketch of The Troubles—the conflict between Protestants and Catholics. They ask me about being Catholic in America, and I tell them my Franciscan church is welcoming of the gay community, and he feels comfortable enough to confide that he and Finn "are together."

We end up laughing about how all Irish families, even ones with watered-down Irish genes, seem to be stocked with secrets. I connect Nora's name to the wife of the great Irish writer James Joyce. I'm ridiculously proud of the fact that Barry is visibly impressed when I brag about how I didn't skip a single word of all 856 pages of *Ulysses*.

"How did you do that, Maureen?" he liltingly jokes.

We only have a few hours before their train returns to Rome. "Have you seen Carlo Acutis?" Maeve asks.

I shake my head. "No, who?"

"The teenager. From Italy. The soccer player who died of cancer. They say more people are coming to Assisi to see him than even Francis."

"Oh! *That's* who that is?" I'd noticed flyers taped on the front windows of the religious tchotchke shops selling all variations of St. Francis and St. Clare. I knew nothing about this boy holding the viewer's gaze, squinting into both the sun and the camera, cropped shiny black curls, the geometric fields of the Italian countryside far below him, and two wide straps of his backpack on either shoulder. Underneath his portrait it read *"Non Io Ma Dio,"* but I didn't know what that meant.

"His body is in Santa Maria Maggiore," Maeve continues. "He died at fifteen, having an extraordinary faith, Maureen. He had spent his life designing a website devoted to recording the hundreds of miracles of the Eucharist. His devotion was of the Real Presence of Jesus in the Eucharist. He wasn't even from a religious family! He went to church every day as a wee child. He's always pictured with his backpack. That's his sign. Do you want to go there with us now?"

"Absolutely."

We gather our things from the table, and I happily follow them down the piazza and through side streets to the church. A crowd chatters inside excitedly despite *"Silenzio"* signs. A white marble coffin, with Carlo inside, is raised up on pillars and illuminated. A homespun wreath of family photos is displayed nearby on the floor. Just like the ritual of a funeral, the images of his holidays, sporting events, all the captured childhood moments are plucked straight from his mother's photo albums.

In the ornate sarcophagus in which he lies, the front panels can slide open and show him in repose. In order to discourage crowds, these panels have been shut during COVID-19. When he was beatified—becoming officially "Blessed," one step short of sainthood—at the Basilica of St. Francis here, over 40,000 came to this town in the course of three weeks. I am relieved I cannot see him in there. Though really, what is the difference between his remains and those of St. Clare in her crypt that I just viewed a few hours ago? That he is simply more recently dead? This veneration in Catholicism fills me with contradictions. I find it shocking, weirdly thrilling, comforting, repellent, and fascinating.

At the end of the room is a life-size cardboard cutout of him with a human-sized chalice and Eucharist. I'm sorry to say it seems tacky to me. Like a cutout you'd have at a high school graduation. Though who am I to judge since he never even got to have a graduation? People are posing in front of the sarcophagus. Mostly Italians, a few international tourists. So many of us wear sneakers to church now, I'm always amazed at the older ladies with big beads who still wear pantyhose and pumps with chunky heels to dress with respect; they kiss their hands then lovingly touch Carlo's marble sides.

Expressing my faith with brand-new friends nourishes me. Back home, I spend a good deal of time in my friendships alone with it, in *silencio*. It's exhilarating to worship together, and because we're all on holiday, it's fun. I'm not shy to bow my head with them as we sit together on a bench. Maeve takes blank sheets of paper and pens near the sarcophagus to write our individual intentions. We scribble, then fold the papers in half and quarters and slip them, with all the others left by people seeking change and healing, into a plastic box, half full. I place my left hand upon his crypt, palm fully open. It's refreshingly cold, soothing the relentless heat of the brokenness I've endured in the dust and screws of my deformed wrist for nearly a decade.

They only have a short time left, they want to see Clare, and we head down to the basilica. Nora and I share that we both wrote intentions for our children.

"It was also very strange, Maureen, because just as I was writing a prayer for her, she called me."

"She felt it," Maeve reassures her.

Walking with them down the street, the men ahead, it seems it's always been this way, the five of us joking around and crossing ourselves unabashedly as we enter churches. It's why I feel that Assisi is my home. I can be the Holy Fool that I am and not think twice about hiding it or defending myself. Beginning my day at one of the basilicas, blessing myself over and over, kneeling and whispering prayers into my woven hands, then I go to San Rufino and bless myself, whisper some more, not caring who sees because no one thinks I'm a weirdo as they, too, are worshiping. They, too, believe. I stop by San Stefano Church in the middle of communion and get in line, then later in the day, walk into Santa Maria while a rosary is being said, and I join in.

Too soon, we must part. Maeve hugs me. "Maureen, come see us in Ireland." How I would love to go, having only been once, but I know there's limited time now in my life to return to the faraway places I've fallen in love with. I'm thinking that, instead of me, I should send Teresita to find the last place her daughter was alive.

I climb back up Via S. Rufino to my apartment and do some research. I have to laugh because, once again I'm the Blind Man not fully seeing. I'll always be a bit of a Mr. Magoo. Apparently, I was just in a church where a powerfully historic event occurred. Carlo Acutis lies in the *Santuario dell Spogliazione*, the Shrine of the Stripping. The site where, in front of his father, Francis threw off his luxurious clothes, renounced the wealth of his family, and stood naked, choosing to follow Christ. No gold, no money, haversack, shoes, no more than one tunic.

I learn the boy's heart is now a relic. Relics: a strange practice, yet I'm transfixed. A piece of Carlo's pericardium, a bit of this sac, is traveling to waiting congregations around the world. So now, while I am in Italy near his bones, a fragment of this beatified boy is back in my country, in New York City. We've crisscrossed on our flight paths.

Whatever one thinks of this practice, and I am not always quite sure myself, I am left with the image of this boy's heart. My heart. The Sacred Heart. The sac that holds our hearts in place in our bodies, enclosing our hearts and the roots of our vessels. There's an outer layer, and an inner double layer; a double doublet within us all.

A relic is defined as something that remains, left over, a portion. Bones, objects, clothing, not just in Christianity, but in Buddhism and Hinduism, too. It can be something kept for sentimental reasons, which makes me think we all have relics. I wonder what you have? What jewelry of loved ones who have passed do you hang on your body, what objects of theirs do you house?

I do understand that the idea of relics, of death or impermanence, creates a desire to look away. Some people never look at it at all. My mother, at eighty-five, is looking. The week before I came to Italy, I went to see her in Maine.

"I might not be here much longer," she said as we toured all the trees in her yard. Should she bother pruning them? "I'm not going to worry about it," she decided as she poked her cane in the center softness of a stump. There was, perhaps, resignation, but not any bitterness in her voice. Just the truth. And surrender.

Later, slumped on her couch with the heating pad relieving the pain of a hairline fracture in her spine, she asked me, "What do people do with all their stuff?" Genuinely wondering as she looked about her home of the last thirty years. All the furniture, books, do-dads. Her husband has died before her, so she now surveyed their sixty-two years together. Upstairs, she placed the urn with my father's ashes, his Purple Heart from Korea, and a black-and-white photo of him lined up, on the top row, holding the American flag for Platoon 80.

I tried to reassure her. I've thought about this quite a bit myself, trying to minimize what my children might have to do for me after I go. "I mean, it's true, Mom, when someone dies, someone has to tend to the stuff after them. Everyone leaves *something* behind, right? Unless we live in a monastery with nothing, but even then, someone has to figure out what to do with the bed."

It's a fairly ridiculous viewpoint, and we laughed.

That night of my visit, I found solitude in the lamplight as my mother slept, and I realized what made her saddest was that the objects in her house had sentimental value. Much of her conversations consist of, "That was my mother's" or "That was Grandma Mann's." Her walls are decorated with the work of her grandmother, framed cross-stitches of strawberries and sparrows with phrases such as *Warm friendship like the golden sun shines kindly light on everyone.* And my favorite, *Leave no tender word unsaid, love while life shall last.*

• • •

And now, in Italy, far from my mother's relics, I'm close to other ones. Assisi's two main churches are the Basilica of St. Francis and the Basilica of St. Clare. In the bottom of each lay the saint's bones. I have been here many days, and the bells ring all day, every fifteen minutes, and are silent at night when I believe these churches, one at each end of the town, are the paperweights holding down the edges of the winds that encircle the earth.

Francis has a double Basilica that, I swear, every sunset, has rays of sun fanning wide from the clouds floating above it (I have proof). The lower Romanesque part was built in 1230, and atop that, the Upper Basilica, Gothic in style, completed in 1239. The whole cathedral borders on ineffable, it surrounds me, soars above me, fills the sky. But I also know the wonder in the little, and in the corner of the ornate lower Basilica, tiny stitches whisper to me from St. Francis' tunic, the one he once wore, protected, pressed flat under glass. Yellow tracks run wildly all over the course brown fabric, covering it in patches and rips, like flaps repaired.

The frescoes inside, by Cimabue and his pupil Giotto, took another hundred years to paint. I go to bask in their energy every morning and night. The church closes at 7:00 p.m. Italians don't heed time like Americans, so the guard is visibly annoyed with me as I slide into the church at 6:50. He's done. The evening has turned cold with rain, and he wants to close up shop. But I have ten minutes! The guard has waved everyone out, sighing, but allows me to slip through.

He doesn't even bother to keep his eye on me, as he wanders out the doors. I look around for silhouettes of people, but there's no one. I am alone. Tourists from all over the world flock here in droves all day, but now, here I am, in the most exalted church in the whole world, and for sixty seconds, I am given the unexpected gift of having this entire basilica to myself. Half the lights are already turned off. Its emptiness I would not describe as quiet or tranquil. What is it? It's *sweet*. It's absolute sweetness.

I am underneath one of the most perfect frescoes ever painted, *S. Francesco riceve le Stimmate*. Francis receiving the stigmata. The wounds of Jesus. Floating above Francis, Jesus is part bird, part angel, arms open, feathered wings spread wide. His face is erased from the two earthquakes that struck, the double tremor, in 1997.

People were tragically killed here, and many of these frescoes were destroyed. It adds to the powerful understanding of impermanence. And fragility.

The guard returns and shoos me out with the Italian word for "closing." He doesn't care that I think this Giotto fresco is beautiful. And I don't care that he doesn't care. I'm emboldened by my glorious stolen moment. I tell him it's beautiful anyway.

• • •

It's midnight. I feel the relics out there, a gilded triptych. Clare, Carlo, Francis. It fills me with the desire to find them, not just while awake but always, even in my dreams. I write to Francis in my journal: *Let me dream tonight of the stitches in your tunic, the knots holding your patches together, let me dream tonight of your arms wide open in the moonlight.*

And the miracles, all of them, move forward, as miracles do, and this new one, a boy who believed, who chronicled miracles about holy bread. Just a kid! Just a kid, a child who gave all he had to God. Until the very end. Perhaps soon to be a saint, who said *Non Io Ma Dio,* which I learn means, *Not Me But God,* perhaps one day a statue in the back of the basilicas, but already guiding us with the straps of his school backpack and his pair of black Nikes.

Fragments of Clare

Basilica of Santa Chiara, Assisi, Italy
(all the words taken from the website in the order they appear, but
some I erased)[8]

The discovery of desire brought to light,
opened, found
within the middle of the tunnel,

the sarcophagus, the remains,
the decrease in bones — only 57 left —
their fragility.

The tissue for a long time,
repeated three times and then as far as possible,
the fragments.

The small remaining shape, dressed,
an opening to her sacred bones,
to make them visible sisters.

The face of St. Clare.
The lips, the precise shape of a mouth, is the true one.
Under the artist's hands, the Mother reborn, an

oval fulfillment.

Marina

Her name means *seashore*, and a place to provide boats with moorings. It's such a fitting name, because the artist residency she's created has provided a harbor for artists from around the world — Spain, South Africa, the U.S., Iran, Cuba, Czech Republic, Venezuela — to immerse themselves in the dream of Assisi. Arte Studio Ginestrelle is two apartments where people stay for weeks with their time centered around their notebooks, watercolors, cameras, gouache, or pencils of graphite. Because of what Marina offers, these weeks have shown me I am a stringed instrument. Assisi has fine-tuned me.

Today she is taking Päivi and me to her olive grove. The three of us walk through the town, the afternoon light so pastel that the swaying wild red poppies are impossible to not stop and photograph. We descend, leaving the town's stone walls behind.

It is tranquil in the countryside. I inhale something sweet in the winds, like climbing jasmine. An occasional car passes us. We grow peaceful inside. The meadows hum with bees and dragonflies. Turning a corner, we're startled by a donkey in an overgrown olive grove who begins to scream. Running as fast as he can toward

Marina, his mouth wide open, gums and teeth exposed, shouting in a raggedy voice, he knows who she is and is going crazy. Päivi and Marina and I cannot stop laughing. He's adorable. From behind an electric fence, he calms down, still snorting, and won't take his eyes off Marina. Clearly, he is in love with her. Pretty much everyone is.

Marina is a very beautiful Italian woman. She has a delicacy in every hour of light, a rosy-peach undertone to her skin. It's curious, because even though she wears a stylish, worn leather biker jacket, it only accentuates her fragility.

She feeds the donkey a few long stems of wild grasses, and on his side of the fence, he trots alongside us until we disappear from view. When we come to her olive grove, I recognize these trees. I've seen this before, in paintings by Van Gogh. He perfectly captured their sage green leaves and the way the trunks and branches darken and twist. She explains to us how in the autumn, nets are spread below, and special rakes pull the olives off, and they tumble to the ground. This is how they are harvested. Then she and her family take the olives to a shop nearby, and the proprietor presses them for the olive oil. I wonder what that olive oil tastes like. I am certain it is beyond delicious.

In Marina's olive grove, at last I understand the Italian way of not keeping track of time. Of not rushing. We settle in, three women talking. I have only known Päivi for a few days, and I enjoy hearing about the project she's working on in the other residency further up the hill. She's from Finland and writes about her Russian grandfather. But since her country borders Russia, ever since the Russian war against Ukraine started a few months back, the support for her work has already been deeply impacted.

I lose myself in the olive grove. It's healing to soak in the magic here, to listen to women. Listen to myself. And the time goes by. I think it has been hours. I can't tell because we are far away from the bells. Marina asks me, "What is your favorite place in America?"

I consider this for a long moment. I have loved Santa Fe and the Outer Banks, but I love New England the best. I love where I live. And I am completely caught off guard to see clearly that I live in my favorite place. It took a trip to another country, to turn around, to admit to the truth of this. I think of the river back home, the fields, the farms. Everyone I meet here in Europe who has been to America or has questions about it, knows that New England is beautiful. When I met Maeve, and told her I lived in New England, her first response was "Fall?" It seems the whole world recognizes the beauty of our autumns.

Eventually we must leave the grove. Our return is a hard, steep walk. But I can see the back of the St. Francis Basilica. And the view of it is just astonishing. How did they build that church in the corner of the town, on that cliff, in the Middle Ages? How did they possibly do it without machinery and cranes? As we climb back to the town, the swallows are dipping in dizzying circles over the poppies. The sun is poised at an angle over the furrows of the Umbrian valley; I can see the farthest I have ever seen while standing with my feet on the ground.

• • •

The day comes when I awake at dawn and climb the stairs to Rocca Maggiore for a final view of the entire town. I cannot bear to part from the bells. In the distance, just a little dot, a hot air balloon rises. I return to my apartment. Marina has come to take the bus with me, to ensure I get on the correct train so that I can make my flight out of Florence in time. First, she gives me a gift, a small clear plastic case with a red rosary from Saint Mary of the Angels.

I remember the first time I came to Assisi, six years ago; she was waiting for me at the station as my train pulled in, as we had planned. I had never met her before. I consider her such a close friend now. We sit on the bench together, talking with a bitter-sweet feeling. I proudly show her photos of me surrounded by my students in their caps and gowns. The train whooshes in. She helps me put my suitcase up on it, and we hug goodbye. I climb up. We blow each other kisses, our tears come. I disappear down the aisle and take my seat. I don't know if she will be standing there when the train begins to move swiftly away, so I wave wildly just in case. She flickers into view, watching for me. She's stricken, as am I. But I'm happy she sees me waving, my final gesture of love as I pull away and we are no longer in each other's sight. I don't know when, or if, Marina and I will ever meet again.

I lift up my backpack and in the front pocket, fish around for her gift. I take the plastic case, flip it open, and pull the rosary out. It's incredibly beautiful and meaningful to me. Not only are the beads shaped like tiny red roses, they also carry their scent. My hands, my whole backpack, become touched with their heady perfume. And because of her question, in my heart I carry this clear vision of home, returning to my favorite place. Funny, I once believed Assisi was my favorite place. I guess I have two.

Moonlight Find

It takes me twenty-four hours to return home, after two weeks away, to a May heat wave. The lily of the valley field outside my house is in full bloom. It's ninety-three degrees and I place my fan in the window. The fragrance of lily of the valley blasts into my room, the sweetness unassailable.

I lie down thinking of where I just was. I feel like I'm in both places at once, remembering how the Calendimaggio festival lasted four days. Drumming all night under my window with the flames lit along the stone walls, the crowd in the piazza cheering the crossbow competition and the choruses and the fire eaters practicing in the tunnels like dragons becoming real in the mouths of men. On the fourth day the townspeople went singing with an accordion player under my window at six in the morning, and I looked down in wonderment at their strength in staying up until dawn together, not even staggering.

The next day Assisi was feathered with the remnants. Broken stems, empty bottles rolling, wooden ox carts decorated with olive branches, long coils of burnt pyrotechnics. Passing the ledge of a stone tunnel, I had spied a spray of bobby pins a costumed woman left behind in putting together her elaborate medieval headpiece. Perhaps that kind shaped like a velvet balloon rising off her head.

I reached over the iron gate and took two of the leftover bobby pins. In the past years I'd purchased pins that had a curve, and didn't stay in and were useless, and pins that were pretty coral until the plastic tips fell off and scraped my scalp and hurt. But these were long and straight, and when I tucked them in, pressed down the flyaways perfectly. I gathered up another pair, slid them up each side behind both my ears. Little relics of the festival. Tiny reminders of finding what we need, and extra. I wore the bobby pins traveling all the way back. But I did not brush my hair on the flights. With a knotted ponytail upon my own pillow, I run my hand through tangled moonlight and find them.

Notes

1. Mark Pepo, *The Book of Awakening* (Newburyport, MA: Red Wheel 2020), 365.
2. Thich Nhat Hanh, *Going Home* (New York: Riverhead, 2000), 164.
3. www.assisisantachiara.it.
4. Betty Smith, *A Tree Grows in Brooklyn*, (New York: Harper Perennial Modern Classics, 2005), 6.
5. Smith, 14
6. John of the Cross, *Spiritual Canticle*, (Garden City, NY: Doubleday Image, 1961), 464.
7. Thérèse of Lisieux, *Story of a Soul*, (Charlotte, NC: TAN Books, 2010), 110.
8. www.assisisantachiar.it.

About the Author

Maureen O'Brien is the author of the spiritual memoir *What Was Lost: Seeking Refuge in the Psalms*. She is a contributor to *St. Anthony Messenger* and the online site *Pause+Pray*. She has also published a novel, *B-Mother* (Houghton Mifflin Harcourt) and *The Other Cradling*, a chapbook of poems (Finishing Line Press). Her award-winning short stories and poems have been published widely in magazine and anthologies. She lives in Connecticut where she taught creative writing to teenagers for twenty-five years. She finds beauty in the contrasts of life—sunrise and dusk, crying and laughter—they never cease to amaze her.